1955

SABRINA FAIR

Sabrina Fair

or

A WOMAN
OF THE
WORLD

A Romantic
Comedy
by
SAMUEL
TAYLOR

RANDOM HOUSE
NEW YORK

Photographs by Vandamm
Jacket photograph of Mr. Taylor
by Bender

For SUZANNE

who taught Sabrina
two things

AUTHOR'S NOTE

There is some question as to the pronunciation of the name Sabrina, and I am not going to try to settle it, now or ever. The vagaries of pronunciation are such that he who attempts to lay down laws had better get ready to run. And as one who pronounced naiveté "na-ee-vet" until the age of eleven, I approach any discussion of this sort with natural caution.

I choose to pronounce Sabrina with the hard, closed, Latin "i," to rhyme with Regina and the Straits of Messina, and it is so pronounced in the American production of this play. Anyone not gainfully employed by The Playwrights' Company is on his own. Those readers who pronounce Regina to rhyme with Dinah-is-there-anyone-finer are having trouble with me already and had best say the hell with it and ask for their money back.

My defense is based on confusion, for both pronunciations are correct by authority and common usage, depending largely on geography and conflicting methods of teaching Latin to the young. But to recognize a confusion is not to resolve it. I say "Don Ju-an" to make Byron scan; in conversation I say "Don Hwon." When reading *Don Quixote* aloud to my children, I say "Don Kee-hoe-tay"; yet I speak of a man who tilts at windmills as being quixotic. Doctor, the windmills keep turning in different directions.

So, let us not try to convert one another. The only letter I have received on the subject is from a gentleman who studied at Princeton and who insists that I am wrong because: a) the inhabitants of Italy are called "Eye-talians (*sic*); and b) John Milton invented the name Sabrina as a deliberate pun so that his water nymph could be called "Sa-brine-uh or the-under-the-water-girl" (*sic*). Both propositions have left me badly shaken, and with a sudden mistrust of higher education in New Jersey. Sabrina was the ancient name of the Severn River, long before Milton was born. And although it is true that the Severn, like all rivers that flow to the sea, has a tidewater estuary, I prefer to think that the poet found his setting for *The Masque of Comus* a little farther upstream, in quieter and less brackish and less controversial waters.

S.T.

SABRINA FAIR *was first presented by the Playwrights' Company at the National Theatre, New York City, on November 11, 1953, with the following cast:*

MAUDE LARRABEE	Cathleen Nesbitt
JULIA WARD MC KINLOCK	Luella Gear
LINUS LARRABEE, JR.	Joseph Cotten
LINUS LARRABEE	John Cromwell
MARGARET	Katharine Raht
DAVID LARRABEE	Scott McKay
GRETCHEN	Ruth Woods
SABRINA FAIRCHILD	Margaret Sullavan
TOM FAIRCHILD	Russell Collins
A YOUNG WOMAN	Harriette Selby
A YOUNG MAN	Gordon Mills
ANOTHER YOUNG WOMAN	Loraine Grover
ANOTHER YOUNG MAN	Michael Steele
PAUL D'ARGENSON	Robert Duke

Directed by H. C. Potter

Setting and lighting by Donald Oenslager

Costume supervision by Bianca Stroock

SCENES

The North Shore of Long Island
about an hour from New York.

ACT ONE
A Saturday afternoon in September.

ACT TWO
Friday evening, two weeks later.

ACT THREE
The following morning.

ACT FOUR
Immediately afterwards.

ACT ONE

PROLOGUE

The music, which is lightly gay and nostalgic and eighteenth century, fades down until it is almost gone.

Out of the darkness in a soft glow, the face of a young girl appears.

THE GIRL *speaks*

Once upon a time,
In a part of America called the North Shore of Long Island,
Not far from New York,
Lived a very small girl on a very large estate.
The house on the grounds had many rooms, and many servants,
And in the garage were many cars,
And out on the water were many boats.
There were gardeners in the gardens,
And a chauffeur to drive the cars,
And a boatman who hauled out the boats in the fall
And scraped their bottoms in winter
And put them back in the spring.
From the windows of her room
The girl could look out on an indoor tennis court
And an outdoor tennis court; an indoor swimming pool
And an outdoor swimming pool
And a pool in the garden for goldfish.
Life was pleasant here,
For this was about as close to heaven
As one could get on Long Island.
But then one day the girl grew up
And went beyond the walls of the grounds
And found the world.

(The light fades out; THE GIRL *disappears; the music is gone.)*

ACT ONE

The scene is a walled garden. The country house it adjoins forms the left wall of the scene, running on a slight angle off down left. Up left, about two-thirds of the way, the house makes a jog out to the right, then runs on upstage. This jog is a small room used as a bar, off the main living room of the house. The main level of the house is above the garden and opens onto a stone terrace about three feet above the ground level. The broad stone steps that lead from the terrace to the garden fit inside the jog, running from the outside wall of the bar downstage some six or eight feet to a graceful iron railing. There is a door from the terrace into the bar facing the audience, and wider, glass French doors in the left wall leading into the main part of the house. The walls are of red brick and indicate a handsome example of a Georgian country house.

This walled garden is rather an open court for living; in Western America it would be called a patio. Upstage, a low red wall topped by gray slate runs from the corner of the house across the stage on a slight angle and off to the right. It is broken just right of center by a wide opening that gives on the gardens of the property. Beyond the opening, two paths diverge, one leading left into the gardens, the other leading right through the gardens and down the hill to the boathouse. We can see only the beginnings of these paths, for we are on a rise of ground. Beyond the brick wall are shrubs and trees; beyond these, the sky and flashing glimpses of Long Island Sound. The scene goes off right to the tennis court and to the garages.

3

Since this garden—this courtyard—is a family gathering place, its furniture is well made and handsome and has an air of permanence.

We are on the edge of Long Island Sound, about an hour from New York City.

It is a Saturday afternoon in September, shortly after lunch; a clear, warm day, with that sparkling brightness peculiar to the seacoast in early autumn.

At rise, the scene seems uninhabited, but then we become aware of the figure of a woman in a chaise longue, the upper half shielded from the sun and from us by the canopy which has been pulled well down. To dispel any mystery immediately, let us say that this is JULIA WARD MC KINLOCK, *a woman of fifty-eight who—it will soon be seen—is plain, stocky, squared-off, with straight gray hair that is cut short, and a plain, square face that shows intelligence and good humor and awareness. At the moment, her most prominent feature is her feet.*

After a short time, MAUDE LARRABEE *wanders up from the garden and appears at the opening in the brick wall up center. She is* JULIA'S *age and is, like* JULIA, *a woman of grace and charm and determination. But there the similarity ends.* MAUDE LARRABEE *has been a reigning beauty all her life, and at fifty-eight gives no sign of abdicating. She is fair and blue-eyed, bright and quizzical, and her smile is a devastatingly effective mingling of laughter and rue. She is slender and small-waisted and erect, with a bearing and a walk that make her seem taller than she is. She has a way of speaking with a wide-eyed candor and directness that make every remark of hers important beyond its meaning and every new experience of hers new—by definition—under the sun. Those wide*

4

*eyes and that impressive directness have helped her im-
measurably to rule her world.*

*Now, as she enters, carrying a basket of freshly cut chry-
santhemums, she instinctively pauses for effect; then, seeing
nothing human other than the lower half of* JULIA's *body, she
crosses to the chaise longue and peers under the canopy.*

MAUDE

Oh! You're awake! Now, Julia, you shouldn't be. (*She
straightens up and pushes the canopy up and back*) My, it
gave me a turn to see those eyes peering out at me. You
looked like a mole in there.

JULIA

I felt like a mole. I was beginning to burrow back.

MAUDE

How far, Julia? Aren't they beautiful? I've never liked fall
flowers—they're so unsettling—but I'm the only one in the
country that has these. (*She crosses over to set the basket
of flowers on the terrace*) John-the-gardener's nephew smug-
gled them out of Japan, and my dear, it was worth his life!
(*Vaguely*) It seems they're sacred to a . . . Celestial Shinto
Garden, or an Exalted Shogun, or . . . you know. I gave
him five dollars. How far back did you burrow, Julia? To
when our hearts were young and gay at Wellesley?

JULIA

Not that far back.

MAUDE

It wasn't that far back.

> (*She crosses back to arrange the throw covering*
> JULIA's *feet.*)

5

JULIA

To when my heart was young and gay, in Paris.

MAUDE

That's quite far enough. (*She smiles reminiscently*) How many years is it, Julia? Thirty? It must be. I remember, you went to Paris the year Warren G. Harding was elected president, and came home the year Franklin D. Roosevelt was elected. How many years between?

JULIA

Hundreds.

MAUDE

(*Ruefully*)

Yes. I've always envied you those years in Paris, Julia.

JULIA

You should. They were wonderful years.

MAUDE

The best years of your life?

JULIA

Yes.

MAUDE

Oh! I was making a joke. Were they really, Julia?

JULIA

Yes. Everything I'd ever wanted to happen to me happened to me then.

MAUDE

Everything?

JULIA

Yes!

MAUDE

(*With a wicked smile of delight as she settles down beside the chaise*)
Why, Julia, you never told me!

JULIA

You never asked me.

MAUDE

Nonsense! I've probably asked you a thousand times. Now come along. We've been best friends for forty years; you might tell me now.

JULIA

I'm still too young and there are still too many people alive. Ask me again ten years from now.

MAUDE

Now you're boasting. (*She discovers the bottle of medicine sitting on the ground*) Have you taken your medicine?

JULIA

I don't need it.

MAUDE

Nonsense! Where's the spoon?
(JULIA *produces it from her lap.* MAUDE *shakes the bottle vigorously.*)

7

JULIA

Maude, I feel fine and have completely recovered from a minor operation.

MAUDE

There is no such thing as a minor operation. Any opening, incision, cut, gash or puncture in the human body not put there by God is a blasphemy and a major disaster.

JULIA

You pierced your ears when you were eighteen.

MAUDE

I was a foolish, wicked girl. (*She takes the pencil from* JULIA) And, Julia, I've asked you not to do any work while you were here.

JULIA

I've got a magazine to get out.

MAUDE

But you're the editor! Why can't you have others do the work?

JULIA

You know, I never thought of that.

MAUDE

You're here to convalesce, and nothing else. And you must admit, this is the place to do it.

JULIA

It certainly is. For a woman who spends her life running up and down Madison Avenue, this is like taking the veil.

You really are safe behind these walls, Maude. The world can't ever get at you here.

MAUDE

Don't talk as though we were isolated. We keep up with the world.

JULIA

Well, you do get the daily papers.

MAUDE

Now, Julia, you love to come here. Admit it.

JULIA

Of course I do. It's always pleasant to visit a place where there are more servants than people. Either pour that stuff or throw it away.

(MAUDE *laughs and shakes the bottle again.*)

MAUDE

All right, my pet. You're paying, now, for all those wonderful, dissolute years in Paris. What started you thinking about it?

JULIA

Paris? I don't know. (*She puzzles over it for a moment*) The girl.

MAUDE

What girl?

JULIA

Your chauffeur's daughter. You said she was arriving home from Paris today.

9

MAUDE

Oh Sabrina. Yes. Strange to think of Sabrina living in Paris for three years.

JULIA

I began to wonder what it was like for her.

MAUDE

Not as it was for you, you can be sure. Sabrina was an earnest, scholarly little mouse, who graduated from a small women's college with all the high honors, and went to Paris for all the wrong reasons. There's so little romance in young people these days, have you noticed, Julia? And so little gaiety. (*She shoves the medicine into* JULIA's *mouth.* JULIA *makes a face.* MAUDE *crosses to the table down left to get a glass of water from the thermos jug*) You went to Paris with the romantic hope that everything you'd ever wanted to happen would happen. And it did. Sabrina went to Paris to be a file clerk in one of those world-saving American projects called NATO, or SHAPE. Wouldn't you know that we Americans would call something that was going to save the world SHAPE? All I can see is a movie star in a low-cut bathing suit, leaning forward.

JULIA

A democratic gesture.
> (LINUS LARRABEE, JR. *appears at the center opening in the back wall. He is in his late thirties, well set up, rugged-looking, and easy in his movements.*)

LINUS

How are you feeling, Aunt Julia?

JULIA

Tiptop.

(*He wanders across the top of the terrace towards the bar.* LINUS *is not at all handsome in the conventional terms, but his features are bold and challenging, and he gives an attractive sense of calm and quiet and reserve. He seems always to be holding himself in, checking his laughter and relishing it alone. He is aware of his power and capabilities; it would take a great deal to shake him. He is dressed in white sneakers, an old pair of gray flannels, and an extremely old and well-worn navy-blue yachting jacket. The shirt is white, but there is no necktie. He wears a battered old blue yachting cap.*)

MAUDE

Oh. Linus. I thought you were out on the Sound.

LINUS

I've been putting the sails on.

JULIA

How's business, Linus?

LINUS

Business is good. How's business with you?

JULIA

Couldn't be better. I read an article about you in *Fortune,* the other day. It said you have organizational know-how.

LINUS

I didn't know it showed. I'll have to speak to my tailor.
(*He goes into the bar.*)

MAUDE

(As she crosses with the glass of water)
Really, this mutual admiration society. Julia, did you know that he flew back from South America the minute he heard you'd gone to the hospital?

JULIA

You don't know the half of it. Every time I rolled over, he had four more doctors standing there. I must have the most expensive incision in history. I think it was the doctor from Boston who hit the jackpot. What was he up to in South America? He wouldn't tell me.

MAUDE

I don't know. I think it had something to do with copper, or tin. It seems one of those governments wasn't being nice about Larrabee Industries, so Linus went down to do something about it. He probably went to start a revolution.

JULIA

Isn't it nice to think my little ulcer may have affected the fate of a nation.

MAUDE

I don't think he'd have dropped his business for anyone but you, Julia.

JULIA

Or you. Or his father. Or his brother. Don't sell your elder son short, Maude. He may not be much a part of the family, but he'll always be around when you want him.

MAUDE

Yes, I know. But isn't it strange, Julia. David is so completely my child; Linus never belonged to me; Linus never belonged to anyone. He's a throwback to some free and independent Larrabee who sailed out of Newburyport in the slave trade and was probably a bit of a freebooter on the side. He walked alone as soon as he could walk.

JULIA

Have you seen much of him lately?

MAUDE

Oh, he comes out week-ends to sail, when he's in this part of the country. And he is good about family dinners.

(*From the house, a peremptory man's voice calls: "Maude! Maude!" and then* LINUS LARRABEE, SR. *appears on the terrace. He is in his late sixties, a spare, slender man of considerable presence and charm. Since he lost interest in most features of his life many years ago, he is inclined to vagueness about occurrences in the present that do not directly concern him, and has become increasingly taciturn, being given to abrupt silences that he shatters abruptly. He carries himself well. He is essentially a courtly and a gracious man.*)

LARRABEE

Maude! Where the devil's Fairchild?

MAUDE

He's gone to meet a train, dear.

LARRABEE

He knows he's to drive me to a funeral.

13

MAUDE

Yes, dear. He'll be back shortly.

LARRABEE

I don't like waiting about.

MAUDE

Now, Linus, you're only going to Oyster Bay. And the funeral isn't until four o'clock.

LARRABEE

I want to get a good seat.

JULIA

How many funerals this week, Linus?

LARRABEE

Two. It's been a damned thin week.

JULIA

Too bad you can't get in a double-header today.
(LINUS *comes out of the bar.*)

LARRABEE

Oh, Linus, Rodney Williams is putting up the Frolic for sale. I said you might be interested.

LINUS

Now, father, what would I want with a hundred-and-six-foot yawl?

LARRABEE

What's wrong with owning a hundred-and-six-foot yawl?

JULIA

That's a good question.

LARRABEE

It is a very good question, Julia. Why should this world we live in make us ashamed to own the things we can afford?

JULIA

I stand on the Fifth Amendment.

LARRABEE

(*To* LINUS)

I told Rodney we'd come over tomorrow and go out with him for the day.

LINUS

I have business appointments tomorrow, Father.

LARRABEE

Tomorrow's Sunday.

LINUS

(*Smiling*)

I sometimes work on Sunday. But I'll tell you what I'll do with you. I'll go out with you tomorrow morning in the sailing dinghies, and race you around the cove, so you can prove you're still the best sailor on Long Island Sound.

MAUDE

(*Brightly*)

Yes, Linus! You'll enjoy that!

LARRABEE

This is serious. The Frolic is the nicest yawl on the east-
ern coast. I don't like to see all the big boats being sold out
of the Sound. You should have a sense of responsibility about
these things.

LINUS

I'm sorry, Father.

LARRABEE

What is it you have to do tomorrow that's so important?

LINUS

Just . . . business.

LARRABEE

Is it the plastics thing?

LINUS

(*Suddenly sharply alert*)
Where did you hear that?

LARRABEE

There's a rumor around that you're going into plastics.

LINUS

(*Sharply*)
Who'd you hear it from?

LARRABEE

Fletcher Boyd. He asked me if it was true.

LINUS

What did you say?

LARRABEE

That I didn't know.

LINUS

That's fine.
(*He wanders away.*)

LARRABEE

I would like to know, from time to time, what goes on in the company that bears my name. Is it true?

LINUS

I'd rather you were able to go on saying you didn't know.
(LARRABEE *crosses to him.*)

LARRABEE

Is that all the answer you'll give me?

LINUS

Yes.
(*Pause.*)

LARRABEE

(*Calmly*)
I am sorry to find your mistrust of the world extends to your father. I will accept the rebuff, since I can do nothing about it. I will say to you that in my world you are admired for the things you do, but not for the way you do them. And I am enough your father to warn you to take care that you never stumble. Because if ever you do, the world will be at your throat.

17

LINUS

I'll remember to wear a stiff collar.

(LARRABEE *turns abruptly and walks into the house.*)

MAUDE

Linus.

LINUS

(*Angry with himself*)

I'm sorry. I'm sorry! I'll make my peace.

(*He runs into the house after his father. The two women look at each other.*)

JULIA

Nothing serious.

MAUDE

No, they even do that over a game of chess. But I wish they wouldn't. Actually, he's proud of his son. But he hates the word "ruthless." And it's so often applied. (*She looks over at the garage impatiently*) I do wish Fairchild would come back.

JULIA

Do I remember her?

MAUDE

Who?

JULIA

The girl. Fairchild's daughter.

MAUDE

Sabrina? I don't know. Do you? You should. She's lived here all her life, over the garage; Fairchild's been our chauffeur for thirty years. Of course you know her, Julia. That dun-colored, sallow little wisp that used to cut around corners when she saw you coming? Very timid, very shy, quite intelligent, and as I recall, terribly athletic. At least, she used to spend most of her time climbing trees. What do you suppose that's a sign of?

JULIA

A vitamin deficiency of some sort. Why is she coming home?

MAUDE

I don't know. Fairchild didn't say. I suppose she got fed up with Paris after three years. She couldn't have had much fun.

JULIA

You didn't give her any letters when she went.

MAUDE

Now, Julia, how could I? Would you write to Madge de Lessac and say, "Dear Countess, this is to introduce my chauffeur's daughter, please give her a whirl?"

(LINUS *appears from the house, at ease again.*)

LINUS

All's well. I've promised to look at that hundred-and-six-foot yawl. (*He smiles wryly*) With a crew of ten. Am I forgiven?

MAUDE

Yes. But I wish you would try not to hit back at him the way you do.

19

LINUS

I can't help it. I always have the feeling he's trying to push me back into the mold. I can't bring his world back by buying a hundred-and-six-foot yawl.

JULIA

No gentleman yachtsman, he.

MAUDE

A little of the gentleman yachtsman wouldn't hurt.

LINUS

I'll try to remember my manners, Mother.

MAUDE

No, I must say you have very good manners.

LINUS

Thank you.

MAUDE

But you do devil your family so.

LINUS

(With a grin)

You tempt me so.
(He kisses her on the top of the head. She sees MAR-GARET, the maid, busy at something within the house.)

MAUDE

Oh, Margaret! Take those flowers, will you? And ask Jessie to fix them and put them in the library. (MARGARET comes out on the terrace, and picks up the basket of flowers.

She is a great bulk of a woman, about fifty years old) Aren't they lovely, Margaret? Tell Jessie she must think of something magnificent to do with them.

MARGARET

Yes, madam.

MAUDE

On second thought, Margaret! Tell her to put them in the living room under me. Under the portrait. And Margaret, while I was in the garden I thought I heard the phone ring.

MARGARET

It was for Mr. Linus, madam. (*And then, though the information has not been sought*) It was Mrs. David Larrabee.

LINUS

(*Coldly*)

You gave me the message, Margaret.

MARGARET

I'm sorry, sir.
> (*And with great dignity, she walks into the house.*
> LINUS *looks across his mother to* JULIA *with a wry smile.*)

LINUS

Here we go again.

MAUDE

Linus, does David know you've been going about with Gretchen quite a bit, lately?

JULIA

(*Quickly*)

Linus, what do I owe you for that operation?

MAUDE

(*Coldly*)

Don't change the subject.

(*She takes the glass of water from* JULIA *and crosses to replace it on the table.*)

LINUS

A lifetime subscription to your magazine. I always forget to pick it up at the newsstand.

MAUDE

Well, Linus? Does David know that you've been going about with Gretchen quite a bit, lately?

LINUS

It's common knowledge, isn't it?

MAUDE

I know. And the servants know. And people who read Cholly Knickerbocker and Mr. Winchell's column, know. I just wondered if David knows.

LINUS

(*Gently*)

I'll be glad to tell him.

MAUDE

After all, he was married to Gretchen.

LINUS

(*With good humor*)

He's not any more. What is it that troubles you, Mother? A man takes out his brother's ex-wife; it certainly isn't incestuous.

MAUDE

It's certainly in questionable taste.

LINUS

Ah, then it's not a matter of morals, it's a matter of etiquette. We don't consult the family priest, we turn to the family bible, Emily Post.

JULIA

Amen.

MAUDE

I hate the new fashion of making fun of the amenities.

LINUS

I'm just trying to get at a basic truth, mother. Am I wrong in going about with Gretchen, or merely wrong in letting it get into the papers? What would you say, Aunt Julia?

JULIA

In matters of this sort, I always ask myself: "What would Lord Byron say?" It puts everything in the proper perspective.

(DAVID LARRABEE *wanders out onto the terrace holding a stop watch on a lanyard.*)

DAVID

Hey, Linus, I've got your stop watch.
> (DAVID *is like* LINUS *in many ways, but is gayer, and at the same time lacks the power, the resolution, and the confidence. He is in his middle twenties. He is slim, fair, and has inherited his mother's grace and looks. He has the easy good humor that marks* LINUS, *and the same way of moving easily, with sure control.*)

LINUS

I'm not racing today, David; just sailing.

DAVID

On the International?

LINUS

No, I put the sails on the Vimsa.

DAVID

I might come along. How are you feeling, Aunt Julia?

JULIA

Bully.
> (DAVID *smiles at his mother.*)

DAVID

I like those flowers, Mother.

MAUDE

Aren't they lovely?

DAVID

They set you off beautifully. Or rather, you set them off beautifully.

MAUDE

Thank you, David.

DAVID

(*To* LINUS)

How soon are you going?

LINUS

As soon as my guest arrives. I don't think it would be any fun for you, David.

DAVID

Oh, have you got a girl coming? (LINUS *nods*) Then you don't want me along. Does she know enough about a boat to handle the ketch with you alone?

LINUS

(*With a glance at his mother*)

Yes, she's pretty good.

DAVID

Then you certainly don't want me along. (*With a knowing grin*) There's hardly any wind. You may never get home.

LINUS

It's a chance I'll have to take.

DAVID

It's a chance you've taken before.

MAUDE

(*Carefully*)

Linus, who is this girl you're taking sailing? Anyone we know?

25

JULIA

(*Cutting in*)

You know, I've been wondering for some time how old you boys have to be before you stop calling me Aunt Julia.

DAVID

What should we call you? Miss McKinlock?

JULIA

Well, my only relationship to you is the fact that I roomed with your mother at college; I think you're old enough now to call me by my first name.

DAVID

Too familiar.

JULIA

I'll settle for, "Hey, you."

LINUS

Too formal.

DAVID

You're stuck with Aunt Julia, Aunt Julia.
(MARGARET *appears on the terrace.*)

MARGARET

Mrs. David Larrabee.

DAVID

(*Startled*)

What?

(GRETCHEN LARRABEE *appears on the terrace, dressed to go sailing. She is* DAVID's *age. She is strikingly, carefully, immaculately beautiful, with the calm air and the hard sheen of a fashion drawing. She is well bred, she is knowing, she is tough.*)

GRETCHEN

Hello. It's so long since I've been here, I thought I should have myself announced. Hello, David, how have you been?

DAVID

(*Puzzled*)
Is there something you wanted to see me about?

GRETCHEN

No. (*She descends the steps and goes to* MAUDE, *addressing* LINUS *as she goes*) I'm sorry I'm late; did you get my message? (*He nods*) Hello, Mother Larrabee. It's wonderful to see you again.

MAUDE

Hello, Gretchen! How nice you look! (*They kiss politely*) Did you drive out from town?

GRETCHEN

No, I'm staying with the Hawkinses, in Syosset. You remember Lisa Hawkins.

MAUDE

Yes, of course! Do you know Miss McKinlock?

GRETCHEN

Yes, of course! (*She crosses to shake hands with* JULIA) Hello, Miss McKinlock, how've you been?

JULIA

Not well. I've had an operation.

GRETCHEN

(*Startled*)

Oh! Oh, I'm sorry (*She glances at* LINUS, *who is enjoying the situation quietly*) You want to go, don't you? (*To* MAUDE) Will I see you when we get back? I'd love to sit and talk for a while.

MAUDE

(*Politely*)

Yes, dear, perhaps we can have a cup of tea. Ask someone to find me.

GRETCHEN

It's so nice to be going out on the Vimsa again. And it's just the way I like it: almost no breeze at all.

(*She smiles at them all and goes out through the garden.*)

LINUS

(*Impassively*)

Well . . .

(*He nods to his mother without expression, then follows* GRETCHEN *into the garden and down the path.*)

DAVID

What the hell's this all about?

MAUDE

(*Embarrassed*)

They're going sailing.

28

DAVID

Why?

MAUDE

They . . . like sailing.

DAVID

Now, come on, Mother, what's going on?

MAUDE

Nothing's going on, David—I don't think. Linus has been
seeing quite a bit of Gretchen lately, and . . .

DAVID

How do you know?

MAUDE

It's common knowledge.

DAVID

Why didn't I know?

MAUDE

You read the New York *Times.*
(*He lets the news sink in, then shakes his head, ruefully.*)

DAVID

Ah, hell! Do you mean he's in the columns again? With
my wife? I suppose everyone knew they were having an
affair except me.

MAUDE

You've no reason to call it an affair, dear.

DAVID

What would you call it?

MAUDE

Well, anyway, she's not your wife.
(*At which* DAVID *has to laugh.*)

DAVID

He brought her here deliberately just to get a rise out of us, didn't he?

MAUDE

Not out of you; out of me. (*Smugly*) But he didn't get it. My, he does have a barbaric sense of humor.

DAVID

Do you think he'll ever settle down to be a sober citizen?

JULIA

He is a sober citizen; he makes a lot of money.

DAVID

Is that your definition, Aunt Julia?

JULIA

Not mine; the world's. He doesn't have to be what you call a sober citizen because he is an unusually productive citizen. He took a settled old American family business and built it into an international empire before he was thirty-five. When a man is enterprising and successful in the things that matter, like money, the world allows him his small eccentricities in the things that don't matter, like women.

DAVID

(*His good humor restored*)

You'd better explain that to Gretchen, because she's going to get taken for a ride.
(*He offers a cigarette to* JULIA.)

JULIA

Forbidden.

MAUDE

Are you sure, David? Gretchen's a clever girl. And she'd give her eye teeth to nail Linus down. She didn't mind divorcing you, so much, since we made it worth her while, but she hated like the devil divorcing our boats.

JULIA

Charming girl.

MAUDE

(*Agreeing*)

Oh, a *very* cold fish. Isn't it sad? So young and pretty. And so very well brought up.

DAVID

(*Easily*)

But not as smart as you think. She wants to be a big operator, and she works at it, but she's an amateur compared to Linus. No girl's ever going to nail him down. You can be sure Linus has been two jumps ahead of her all the way along—and laughing. He hasn't made a false move since he was three.

(*A pause as he smiles, thinking of* LINUS.)

JULIA

(*Abruptly*)

David, do you dislike your brother?

MAUDE

Why, Julia! What an idea!

31

DAVID

(Smiling)

I remember reading about that in college, Aunt Julia. What is it they call it among you intellectuals? Sibling rivalry?

JULIA

That's right. It's all the rage among us intellectuals.
(LARRABEE *comes out of the house, looking at his watch.*)

DAVID

I like him more than any man I've ever known. I always have.

LARRABEE

Who's this you're so fond of?

DAVID

My brother.

LARRABEE

That's a praiseworthy sentiment, David. But it's not the sort of thing one says out loud. Where is Linus? I want to talk to him about the yawl.

MAUDE

He's gone sailing with Gretchen.

LARRABEE

Gretchen? David's Gretchen?

MAUDE

Well . . .

LARRABEE

(*Affably*)

I haven't seen Gretchen in some time, David. Where have you been keeping her?

MAUDE

Linus, David and Gretchen are divorced.

LARRABEE

Oh. Oh, yes. (*To* DAVID) Why did you do that?

DAVID

We discovered we didn't like each other.

LARRABEE

I should think you could have discovered that without getting married. What's she doing here?

DAVID

She's gone sailing with Linus.

LARRABEE

Well, you can't object to that; he's the best sailor on Long Island Sound. (*To* MAUDE) Why did he go to the station?

MAUDE

(*Startled*)

Who?

LARRABEE

Fairchild.

MAUDE

To meet his daughter. You remember, dear. Sabrina was arriving this morning, on the *Ile de France*.

33

LARRABEE

Sabrina. Is Fairchild's daughter named Sabrina? I thought it was Della.

MAUDE

No, Della was her mother, our cook.

LARRABEE

Oh, yes. I miss Della.

MAUDE

So do we all.

LARRABEE

But it was a good funeral. We gave it just the right tone: simple, unpretentious, but dignified.

JULIA

No cook could ask for more.

MAUDE

(Quickly)

Linus, don't you think you could drive yourself to the funeral this afternoon? It seems a shame to drag Fairchild off as soon as he gets home, when he hasn't seen his daughter in three years.

LARRABEE

Three years. Why would anyone want to live in Europe for three years?

JULIA

I'll be glad to answer that question.

34

MAUDE

It's no effort to drive to Oyster Bay, Linus. Why don't you take David's little English car? You enjoy driving it so.

LARRABEE

(With cold precision)

Maude: Lyman Ward, who was my friend and who now lies dead in Oyster Bay, once observed that man's progression through this world is a series of indignities. He is born in an undignified manner, is married as an insignificant part of a female ritual, procreates in a grotesquely undignified position, and spends the rest of his life being ignored by his issue. In the light of this it was Lyman's belief—and it is mine—that it is a man's duty and the duty of his friends to see to it that his exit from this world, at least, shall be made with all possible dignity. It is very little, but it is all that is left. I do not, therefore, propose to drive up to the church in Oyster Bay for Lyman Ward's funeral dressed in white flannels and a school blazer, perched up in an English two-seater. *(He starts for the bar)* How do you feel, Julia?

JULIA

Rrrripping.
(He goes into the bar. MAUDE looks after him with amused affection, then smiles at DAVID.)

MAUDE

I hope you can do that when you're seventy.

DAVID

So do I.

MAUDE

My, when I think of him as he was in the early years . . .
(*She smiles, thinking back*) There was a time when people
knew how to talk, and dinner parties were exciting . . .

JULIA

He's not seventy, is he?

MAUDE

He will be, in January. Julia, I think you should let up on
Linus a bit.

JULIA

In what way?

MAUDE

You catch him up on all the little things he says that he
doesn't really mean; you always have.

JULIA

It's because he means them. Your husband is one of the
wittiest men I've ever known. He is also one of the stuffiest.

MAUDE

(*Denying it*)

Oh!

DAVID

Can the two go together?

JULIA

They can and they do. It is possible to find the world funny
and not one's self. If anyone else went trotting off to every
funeral he could find, like a morbid bird dog, your father
would have something quite sharp to say about him, I'm
sure.

36

MAUDE

Morbid! He's not a bit morbid, Julia! When he gave up
sailing, and sold the schooner, his doctor told him he ought
to take up another hobby, so he took up going to funerals.
There's nothing morbid about that.

JULIA

No, no. Sort of gay.

MAUDE

It gets him out among people. And it keeps him out in the
open air; he always goes along to the cemetery.

JULIA

(*To* DAVID)

Your mother is the only person I know who can make a
preoccupation with death sound like good, clean fun.

MAUDE

Oh, what nonsense! Preoccupation with death, indeed!
Come take your nap. I can always tell when you're tired;
you begin to sound like the voice of doom. (*She starts haul-
ing* JULIA *out of the chaise longue and* DAVID *hurries to help*)
I'll never forget the fashion article she wrote that began:
(*She quotes with foreboding*) "Women's fashions, this fall,
will reflect the tensions of the times." I went right out and
bought six frivolous hats. David, get the medicine.

JULIA

(*With good humor, as she and* MAUDE *start for the house*)
Thank you, Maude, I prefer to walk alone.

    (MAUDE *ignores this, and puts her arm through* JULIA's
    as though it were the most natural thing in the world.
    They get part way across when they are arrested by a
    call from off right. A young feminine voice, bright

and excited, calls "Hello!" eagerly. They stop and
turn and look off to the right, and once again the call
comes, almost anxiously this time: "Hello!")

MAUDE
(Puzzled)

Who's that?

(And as if in answer, the owner of the voice runs onto
the scene. SABRINA FAIRCHILD *is about* DAVID'S *age,*
and will look very much as she does now when she is
very much older; for she is one of the lucky ones in
whom youth and age will never be measured by days
and years. She is beautifully and tastefully and ex-
pensively dressed in traveling clothes that show off a
very good figure. No one could look more chic. She
is not pretty, but her face is appealing and bright with
animation and reflects the inner glow of a girl in love;
for SABRINA FAIRCHILD *has fallen in love with the*
world and is carrying on a passionate affair with it.
Now, as we first see her, her face is a galaxy of com-
plicated emotions. She is eagerly happy to see these
people whom she adores, but she is shy, too, for they
are not her family, and the past three years have not
altogether dissipated the shyness that was ingrained
from childhood. This trace of shyness, however, is not
apparent to the people who watch her come towards
them. She goes directly to MAUDE.)

SABRINA

Oh, hello! Oh, I'm so glad to see you!

(And she stops dead in front of MAUDE *with a great*
smile of anticipation, and waits to be greeted in re-
turn.)

MAUDE

(*Tentatively, after a moment*)

Sabrina . . . ?

SABRINA

(*Brightly*)

Yes, of course!

MAUDE

(*Just as brightly*)

Yes, of course! It's Sabrina! Why, Sabrina, I didn't recognize you! Welcome home, my dear!

(*She puts out her hands, and* SABRINA *takes them enthusiastically.*)

SABRINA

Oh, I was hoping you wouldn't recognize me! Have I changed? Have I really changed? (*She backs up a bit, hanging on to* MAUDE's *hands*) I'm so glad to see you! David, you didn't recognize me, either did you? (*He shakes his head, fascinated*) Ah! Then I have changed, haven't I? I don't mean just the clothes, that's easy. But me! Myself! Do I seem very different? Here! Now! Without the hat! (*And she tears off the smart, ridiculous little hat, and shakes out her hair*) Now!

MAUDE

(*A bit shell-shocked*)

Now more than ever.

SABRINA

How wonderful! I wanted to hear you say that. Is that vain of me? I don't mean it to sound vain. But I thought it would be such fun to hear you say it. Because I *feel* so different! It was the first thing I thought of when I woke up this morning, as the ship was coming up the bay. And then later,

39

lying in my berth, having breakfast—my last breakfast of that good French bread and that horrible coffee that I love so—I thought: (*She closes her eyes and tells her dream, with a soft smile*) what fun it will be . . . they'll all be in the garden, in the walled garden off the terrace . . . and I'll come running in to them to say hello. And they'll say: "Sabrina? Is it Sabrina? Why, Sabrina, we didn't recognize you!" (*She opens her eyes and grins*) And that's the way it happened! Ah! I think if you had just said, "Oh, hello, Sabrina, how are you?" I'd have died. (*She whirls on* JULIA) You don't remember me, but I remember you. I used to peek around corners at you.

JULIA

I remember you very well. You used to climb trees, too.

SABRINA

Yes, I did. You're famous in Paris, did you know that? I kept hearing about you all the time. It seems as though everybody knows you. And they tell such wonderful stories about you, in the twenties: about you and Picasso and Gertrude Stein, and the book shop you ran, and the magazine . . . It must be fun to be part of a legend.

JULIA

I think the legend has been exaggerated a bit over the years.

SABRINA

Oh, no! Paris was the most exciting place in the world, then, wasn't it?

JULIA
(*Smiling*)

Yes, it was.
(*She likes this girl very much.*)

40

SABRINA

It still is. (*She turns and yells*) Father? (*Her father has appeared from the garage court, dressed in chauffeur's livery,
carrying his cap and* SABRINA'S *topcoat.* TOM FAIRCHILD *is a
stocky, gray-haired man of fifty-five, and at this moment he
looks uneasy. A slim book of the Modern Library-Every-
man's Library sort sticks up out of his coat pocket*) I wish
you could have seen Father at the station. He was completely baffled. There I was, charging across the platform
at him, yelling, "Father!", and he kept looking over his
shoulder to see who my father was! (*She crosses to him
swiftly, smiling at him lovingly*) I finally had to leap at him
to make him recognize me, didn't I, Father? And the most
terrible thing happened! I leaped too hard and knocked him
down! Right there in front of all Glen Cove! Father! The
most dignified man on Long Island! (*She gives him an affectionate peck on the cheek*) Thank goodness it wasn't a com-
muters' train.

FAIRCHILD
(*Coldly*)

Put on your hat, Sabrina.

SABRINA

Oh! (*She looks over to the others anxiously*) Am I being
too . . . too . . .

MAUDE

No, dear, of course not.

SABRINA

It's just that I'm so excited. (*With rueful humor, softly, to
her father*) I'm sorry, Father. I shall keep my place as soon
as I know it. But for now, do be an angel and get that thing
out of the station wagon for me. You know: the . . . (*She

secretly mouths the word "bird" at him, and urges him off)
. . . I want to give it to her now. And be careful of it, please!
(*She watches him go, with a fond smile, then turns back to*
MAUDE) . . . I brought you something from Paris. Do you
mind? It was given me by a beau, and I fell madly in love
with it. And then I knew I would have to bring it home to
you.

MAUDE

You shouldn't have, Sabrina.

SABRINA

I know. But I wanted to.

MAUDE

I should think your beau would mind.

SABRINA

No. I told him. He didn't mind after I told him about you.
(*With deep affection*) It's something I hope will make you
laugh. I wanted to bring it to you because I remembered how
you laughed and how I loved so to hear you when I was a
little girl.

MAUDE

Oh.

SABRINA
(*Softly*)

Isn't it strange of the English language, and typical, that
there is no feminine analogue of "hero worship?"

MAUDE
(*Moved*)

That's very sweet, Sabrina.

(LARRABEE *appears on the terrace.*)

42

LARRABEE

Fairchild? Maude, what the devil's become of him?

MAUDE

He'll be with you in a moment, Linus. He's just returned.

LARRABEE

I'd planned to be started by now.

SABRINA

Hello, Mr. Larrabee!

LARRABEE

Good afternoon, Gretchen. I'm delighted to see you again.

MAUDE

Now, Linus, does she look like Gretchen?

LARRABEE

Since I haven't the faintest recollection of what Gretchen looks like, I couldn't say. Who are you, young lady?

SABRINA

Sabrina Fairchild!

LARRABEE

Sabrina? Really? (*He looks at* MAUDE; *she nods*) You must forgive an old man, Sabrina. I have reached that sad period of old age when all pretty young women look alike.

SABRINA

How very sad for the young women, sir.

43

LARRABEE

(*Impressed*)

Will you come a little closer, please? (SABRINA *darts across and stops before the steps*) I would *like* to remember you the next time I see you. (*He glances at* MAUDE) No one like this ever lived over our garage. (SABRINA *laughs*) But if you say you are Sabrina, I must believe you. And I am happy to see you back, Sabrina. Now, will you tell your father I am waiting for him, my dear? And ask him to bring the big car around.

(*He nods and goes into the house, leaving* SABRINA *with the laugh hanging. She turns back to the others a little shaken, but recovers quickly.*)

SABRINA

He sold his schooner, didn't he? Why did he sell it?

MAUDE

He decided there was no one left to sail with.

SABRINA

Oh?

DAVID

(*Easily*)

Father has always explained to us that you can do business with anyone, but you can only sail a boat with a gentleman.

SABRINA

(*Blithely*)

How lonely you must be! Ah, there it is! (*She skips across the stage, calling*) I'll take it, Father! Mr. Larrabee wants you! You're to bring the big car around right away! (*By now she is offstage, but we can still hear her*) And please don't

44

worry about me. I'll be all unpacked and respectable when you get back.

(MAUDE *and* DAVID *are watching her.*)

MAUDE

What is that she has?

DAVID

It looks like a cage.

JULIA

Don't tell me she's brought you her beau.

(SABRINA *runs on, and it is a cage she carries: a great, magnificently rococo white wire bird cage out of the nineteenth century. Within the cage, calm, proud, sedate, sits a brilliantly colored cockatoo.*)

SABRINA

Here he is! Isn't he beautiful? His name is Maurice.

MAUDE

Sabrina, how beautiful!

DAVID

I never saw a parrot like that.

SABRINA

No, a cockatoo. And the most beautiful cockatoo in the world, aren't you, *mon chouchou*? Do you like him? Ah, but I haven't told you! He doesn't talk; not a word. He sings! Yes! He has a beautiful whisky tenor. Oh, I do hope you like him!

MAUDE

But what a magnificent gift, Sabrina! I should think it would break your heart to give him up!

45

SABRINA

Ah, no, I want you to have him. Please. He'll be such fun for you. He's terribly bright, and he loves to sing. Maurice, this is your new mistress. Will you sing for the lady?

JULIA

What does he sing?

SABRINA

Nursery songs! He has a marvelous repertoire of French nursery songs. I don't know where he learned them. But you haven't lived until you've been wakened in the morning by a cockatoo, singing: (*She sings*) *"Il était un' bergère, Et ron ron ron, Petit patapon . . ."* Come on, Maurice! *"Il était un bergère, Qui gardait ses moutons, ron ron, Qui gardait ses moutons."*

(*She waits expectantly.*)

THE BIRD

Aaaarrk.

DAVID

He needs tuning.

SABRINA

He's shy, that's the trouble.

JULIA

He's French, that's the trouble. Do you usually speak English to him?

SABRINA

No, of course not! That's it! Really, how stupid. (*She turns back to the bird, and in fluent, darting French addresses him*) *Ah, mon p'tit, ça te gêne devant les Américains, n'est-ce pas?*

Comme je suis bête! Mais, ne t'inquiète pas, mon trésor.
(MAUDE *looks at* JULIA *with raised eyebrows, impressed by
the girl's fluency*) *Cette belle dame qui sera ta maîtresse est
adorable! Regards-la! Une vraie duchesse! Et riche! Oh! C'est
fantastique! Tu auras une vie formidable! Et maintenant, tu
vas chanter un peu, n'est-ce pas?* (*By now, the three specta-
tors are caught up by the intensity of* SABRINA'S *pleading, and
are pulling for the bird to join her in song.* SABRINA *sings,
beating out the time with a clenched fist*) "Sur le pont
d'Avignon, l'on y danse, l'on y danse, Sur le pont . . ." (*She
waits. Silence from the bird*) Maurice! (*He grooms himself*)
Oh, dear, I could cry! Honestly! He sings like a bird!

DAVID

I wondered about that.

MAUDE

Do you suppose I intimidate him?

SABRINA

How could you?

JULIA

Of course you intimidate him! He doesn't know anything
about you. Except that you're rich. Speak to the bird.

MAUDE

Bonjour, Maurice.

SABRINA
(*Hopefully*)

He might sing if *you* started a song for him, just to make
him feel at home.

47

MAUDE

(*Retreating*)

Oh, I hardly think . . .

DAVID

(*Amused*)

Yes, that's obviously what he's waiting for, Mother.

JULIA

Go ahead, Maude.

MAUDE

Well . . . does he know this one? (*She sings*) "*Au clair de la lune . . .*"

SABRINA

Of course!

MAUDE

"*Mon ami Pierrot, Prête-moi ta plume, pour écrire . . .*" (*No co-operation from the bird. She gives up.*)

JULIA

Here, let me try. (*She approaches the cage and addresses the bird firmly*) *Ecoute, mon vieux! Pas de blagues! Je te connais bien, toi! Je veux que tu chante avec moi, tu comprends? Eh bien! Allons-y!* (*She sings*) "*Auprès de ma blonde . . .*"

MAUDE

Julia! That is not a nursery song!

JULIA

It always seemed to me as though it should be. Besides, I suspect this bird of hidden talents. *Alors, mon vieux!* "*Auprès de ma blonde, Qu'il fait bon fait bon fait bon, Auprès de ma blonde . . ."*

> (*She stops as she sees* SABRINA *staring past her to the terrace.* MARGARET, *the maid, stands there holding a sweater.*)

SABRINA
(*Lovingly*)

Ah, Margaret!

MARGARET
(*Not quite sure*)

Sabrina?

> (SABRINA *dashes across and up the steps, and throws herself into the woman's arms.*)

SABRINA

Ah, Margaret, I'm so glad to see you!
> (*Margaret drops the sweater.*)

MARGARET

(*Holding her close, letting the tears flow without reserve*)
Sabrina . . .

SABRINA
(*Mistily*)

Yes, Margaret, I'm home . . . I've come home . . .

MARGARET

You were so far away!

SABRINA

I know. But I'm home now. Don't cry, Margaret. It isn't anything to cry about, is it?

MARGARET

And you've come home such a beautiful lady!

SABRINA

Please don't cry, Margaret.

MARGARET

No, no, I'll be stopping now. (*She makes an effort to pull herself together, and looks over at* MAUDE) I beg your pardon, madam. (*But another look at* SABRINA *brings on new freshets*) My little Brina . . .!

> (SABRINA *puts an arm about her and leads her into the house.*)

SABRINA

(*As they go*)

Come along, now. I want to see Jessie and the others. You look wonderful, Margaret. You *have* lost weight! And I loved your letters so! I've brought you all the things you asked for. And a lovely handbag to go with your black satin. And oh, Margaret, a hat! A real Paris hat for you to wear to church on Sundays! Wait 'til you see it! It's the most beautiful hat!

> (*She laughs at the memory of the hat, and without a backward glance at the others, completely intent on* MARGARET, *she leads the woman into the house. The three look after them, saying nothing. Finally:*)

MAUDE

(*Moved*)

She does look like a lady.

JULIA

She may even be a lady.

MAUDE

(*Flaring*)

Oh, Julia, don't be such a woman of the people! You know very well what I meant.

JULIA

(*Grinning*)

Tell me, Mrs. Larrabee, have you any more dun-colored, sallow little mice growing up in odd corners of the property?

MAUDE

Julia, I swear that's the way she was. Wasn't she, David? She *was* shy.

DAVID

Yes, she was. She knew me well because we're about the same age, but she was frightened to death of Father, and a little of Linus, and she was especially shy with you, because she adored you. You were the Lady in the Picture on the Wall; you were the Fairy Princess. It looks as though you still are.

(SABRINA *appears on the terrace, running, dashes down the steps and off to the right, out of sight.*)

SABRINA

(*As she runs, never stopping*)

Excuse me. Margaret wants to see her hat.

JULIA

(*After* SABRINA *is gone*)

Maude? Whatever vitamin deficiency she may have had as a child has been corrected.

MAUDE

I think it's glandular. And I'd love to know which gland. (*The two women start for the house*) Do you like her, David?

DAVID

I won't know till she stands still.

MAUDE

I *like* her. And I'd love to know about those past three years in Paris. When a girl blossoms like that, you can be sure there's a man somewhere in the background. Or men.

DAVID
(Interested)

Oh?
(The women stop to look back.)

MAUDE

My! Look at her run!

JULIA

I don't think any man could catch her.
(She goes in.)

DAVID
(Grabbing the cage)
Mother, don't go off without your new friend.

MAUDE

Now, David.

DAVID

Come on, Mother. You haven't lived until you've been awakened in the morning by a singing cockatoo.

MAUDE
(Taking the cage)
I've managed so far. Well . . .
(She goes into the house, watching the bird warily. A moment, then SABRINA runs on, carrying a Paris hat box. DAVID manages to be in her way.)

52

DAVID

Idle down to forty. Your carburetor needs adjusting.

SABRINA

(*Laughing*)

I know. Isn't it terrible? I can't stop. You should have been there at the station when I knocked Father down. (*She winces at the memory*) People picked me up and dusted me off, and I was so rattled, all I could say was: "It's all right, he's my father!" It does sound idiotic, doesn't it? But you know what I meant. It's perfectly permissible to knock down your father, but you never knock down your chauffeur.

DAVID

Oh, I agree! It's one of the first things you learn.

SABRINA

(*Lovingly*)

Ah, David!

DAVID

(*Smiling down at her*)

Glad to be home?

SABRINA

(*Overflowing*)

Oh!!!

DAVID

You have changed.

SABRINA

It's been a long time, David. Especially for us. Do you know how many years? I was away at college when you went off to the wars, and when you came back, I had gone off to Europe. We're almost strangers.

DAVID

We'll soon fix that.

SABRINA

(*With more affection than she would care to know she shows*)
You look well, David. And so mature. You're the kind
that improves with age.

DAVID

Any gray hairs?

SABRINA

(*Grinning*)
Oh, when you're gray, you'll be irresistible. Isn't it odd,
David? We *are* strangers. The only common experience we
had was living here and playing together as children, but
that's been gone a long time. We've been to opposite ends
of the world . . . you've had a war . . . and a marriage
. . . and a divorce . . . (*She smiles at him gently*) I'm
sorry about the divorce, David.

DAVID

So am I.

SABRINA

I thought of you on your wedding day. It was a Saturday,
and I was in the country, at Saint Germain en Laye, walking
down a long *allée* of trees, and I thought: right now he's
walking up the aisle . . . with her.

DAVID

I'm sorry you weren't there.

SABRINA

No, I didn't want to be.

54

DAVID

Why?

(*A small pause.*)

SABRINA

I liked your wife in the picture I saw. She had . . . distinction. I hoped I would meet her one day.

DAVID

You can; she's here.

SABRINA

Oh, with Linus?

DAVID

Now, how did you know about that?

SABRINA

About Linus and your wife? It's common knowledge.

DAVID

Even in Europe?

SABRINA

(*Laughing*)

Ah, no! But I've been kept informed. I've had a faithful correspondent: Margaret. And I know everything that's happened in this house even to the number of champagne glasses broken last New Year's Eve. I know all about *you*. Every move you've made.

DAVID

Every move?

SABRINA

Almost every move.

55

DAVID

Margaret must have written very long letters.

SABRINA

She did. I insisted.

> (*They are smiling at each other with easy familiarity.* LINUS *wanders on. He does not see* SABRINA, *for she is blocked off by* DAVID.)

LINUS

David, you haven't seen a sweater lying around here, have you?

DAVID

A sweater? No.

LINUS

Gretchen thinks she may have left it here. Oh.

> (*He sees the sweater on the terrace, picks it up and starts out.* SABRINA *looks up at* DAVID *with a wicked smile of "here I go again," darts over to* LINUS, *and stands before him challengingly.*)

SABRINA

Hello.

LINUS

Oh, hello, Sabrina, how are you?

> (*She sucks in for a moment, then, with a small set of the mouth, slams him in the middle with the hat box, turns and darts up the steps and into the house.* LINUS *doubles over, soundlessly.* DAVID *collapses with laughter.*)

The Curtain Falls

ACT TWO

ACT TWO

A Friday evening two weeks later. The same walled gar-
den in moonlight. There are areas of shadow that the moon
cannot dissipate and that the light from the house cannot
quite penetrate. The house is brilliantly lit; there is a party
in progress. A four-piece orchestra of that peculiar kind that
plays only at house parties, and that seems always to be
playing at a house party of the twenties, is making its way
warily through Gershwin's "Someone To Watch Over Me."

At rise: MR. LARRABEE *stands on the terrace looking out*
toward the garden. He wears a dinner jacket and holds a
drink in his hand. After a moment, he calls out.

LARRABEE

Linus? (*He waits, then tries again*) Linus!
    (*But obviously his heart is not in it.* MRS. LARRABEE, *in*
    evening dress, appears from the house.)

MAUDE

Have you found him, Linus?

LARRABEE

No.

MAUDE

Did you look in the bar?

LARRABEE

Yes.
    (*He takes a drink.*)

MAUDE

Really it's wrong of him to disappear like this. Poor Mar
Townsend looks stricken, and is trying desperately to act a
though nothing had happened.

LARRABEE

I can't see that anything very much has happened. Yo
threw a girl at his head and he ducked.

MAUDE

I trust you're not defending your son's manners.

LARRABEE

No, merely his taste. (*He calls*) Linus?
(JULIA, *in evening dress, comes out of the bar, and the
door bangs behind her. She carries a champagne glass
filled to the brim.*)

JULIA

He's not in the bar.

MAUDE

Julia, that *is* ginger ale, isn't it?
(JULIA *looks at her warily, examines the drink carefully, then takes a small, tentative sip, and tastes and
considers.*)

JULIA

(*Doubtfully*)
It's been so long since I *had* ginger ale . . .

LARRABEE

No reason why she shouldn't have a drink. Alcohol's a pre-
servative.

MAUDE

I don't recall that the doctor said she needed pickling. Do
go look for him, Linus.

LARRABEE

Maude, I am too old to be a father. And even at my best, I
was not equipped to be Linus' father. You'll excuse me, my
dear.

> (*He goes into the house, passing two young people
> who come dancing dreamily out onto the terrace,
> slowly, their eyes closed.* MAUDE *stares out into the
> garden grimly, her jaw set.*)

JULIA

Give it up. It's not that important.

MAUDE

It is to me.

JULIA

To get Linus married? Why?

MAUDE

I don't want any son of mine to become a lecherous old
bachelor.

JULIA

I know a lot of married men who are lecherous old bache-
lors.

> (*With great anticipation she starts to raise the glass
> to her lips. The dancing couple bumps into her arm;
> the champagne spills on the ground.*)

THE GIRL

Oh!

THE BOY

Oh, I'm terribly sorry!

JULIA

(*Grimly*)

Everybody's against me.
(*She goes back into the bar.*)

THE GIRL

(*Calling*)

Did it get on your dress?

MAUDE

No, it didn't, dear.

THE BOY

I'm sorry, Mrs. Larrabee, we didn't see you.

MAUDE

Perfectly all right, Peter. Dancers have the right of way, this evening. (*She smiles at the girl*) Are you having a good time?

THE GIRL

Yes, it's a wonderful party.

MAUDE

That's a pretty dress. (*She starts for the house*) Peter, if you should happen to stroll down to the boathouse, will you look about for Linus? And if you see him, tell him we're about to go in to supper.

THE BOY

(*Innocently*)

Oh, we won't be going down to the boathouse, Mrs. Larrabee.

(MAUDE *smiles and goes into the house. The two young people look at each other with slightly lifted eyebrows and slightly challenging smiles, then begin to dance again. They move into an area of shadow, and their movements become smaller and smaller until they are standing still in the archway in the attitude of the dance. Finally they give up all pretense, adjust their arms to a more comfortable position, and lock in a close embrace. Finally, they part*)

Come on.

THE GIRL

Not the boathouse. I'll be cold.

THE BOY

No you won't. Come on.

THE GIRL

No, the boathouse is cold at night.　·

THE BOY

Well, there's a little house at the end of the rose garden, they call "The Hideaway." Nobody ever goes there. Come on.

(*They hurry off into the garden.*

LINUS, *in a dinner jacket, appears in the archway from the other direction, and watches them go with a small smile. The orchestra inside the house stops playing with a small fanfare to indicate that the dancing is ended for the time being, and that supper is about to begin.* LINUS *turns down from the archway, and is about to wander onto the terrace, when he sees someone coming from the direction of the garage. He retires into the shadow of the archway again. A moment, then* SABRINA *appears, and walks on slowly. She wears a simple dress and carries a sweater. She stands quietly looking at the house, then leans on the wall and watches the activity within.*

Her father, FAIRCHILD, *appears from the garage, obviously looking for her. He holds a volume of Everyman's Library, with a finger inserted to hold his place. He looks about, sees her, and moves to her.*)

FAIRCHILD

Sabrina . . . (*She gives the faintest indication that she hears him*) . . . Sabrina, what are you doing?

SABRINA

(*With a small smile*)
Watching the rich folk, pappy.

FAIRCHILD

I thought you were going to a movie.

SABRINA

I did. I went in to Oyster Bay, and then had a soda at the drug store. Howard Whitman, who went to school with me, was behind the fountain, and he put in an extra scoop of vanilla and asked me if I'd hang around until he knocked off work. What's happened to the music?

FAIRCHILD

Come home, Sabrina. I don't like you doing this.

SABRINA

I always used to do it, Father. And it was always such
un. I used to sneak down in my bathrobe and listen to the
music and see them all so beautifully dressed. And next day
at lunch I had a piece of the cake. Mother saved it for me;
then, after Mother died, Margaret saved it for me. But the
important thing is that I always had a piece of the cake.

FAIRCHILD

(*Uncomfortably*)

It's different now.

SABRINA

In what way different, Father? Margaret will save me a
piece of the cake, I'm sure. Nothing has changed here.

FAIRCHILD

(*Accusingly*)

You've changed!

SABRINA

(*Flatly*)

Well, they're changing me back.

(LINUS, *unseen, retires behind the wall of the archway.*)

FAIRCHILD

No, not to the way you were. You were such a nice, quiet
girl. How could anyone change so much in five years? You
were so likable!

65

SABRINA

Oh, Father! Don't you like me now?

FAIRCHILD

(*With a mounting sense of injury*)

It's been very upsetting having you home, Sabrina. In just two weeks you've upset everybody: me, Margaret, John, Jessie. You have something to say about everything. You want everybody to *do* something. Why should Jessie go to the Metropolitan Museum of Art on her day off? Her feet hurt enough!

SABRINA

I'm sorry! I didn't think of her feet!

FAIRCHILD

Well, you should have!

SABRINA

Yes, I should have. But you needn't fear, Father. Paris will wear off. Cinderella's been to her ball, but now she's back in the chimney corner, and no Prince Charming to seek her. (*Ruefully*) Anyway, I've got such *big* feet.

FAIRCHILD

What's the matter, Sabrina?

SABRINA

(*In a burst*)

I'd know what to do if they were rude, but I can't cope with being ignored! I just don't know how!

FAIRCHILD

They talked about inviting you. Margaret heard them. I didn't see any reason to tell you. *She* was talking to *him,*

and she said she didn't think it would be fair to you to ask
you because you'd feel strange among all these people you
didn't know.

SABRINA

That was considerate. And what did *he* say?

FAIRCHILD

I don't know.

SABRINA

I can guess. And still I was invited. By David. But then
he laughed and said his mother disapproved, and I declined
with thanks. (*She smiles at her father*) Don't worry, Father,
I didn't embarrass him. I made up a very good excuse that
I've forgotten now.

FAIRCHILD

(*After a long pause, gently*)
Sabrina, I think you ought to go away again.

SABRINA

(*Far away*)
So do I. But where shall I go? I came home from Paris to
find out something about myself, and no one's given me a
chance to find out. The only thing I've learned is that this
isn't home. Where shall it be? If I'm a girl without a home,
am I a girl without a country? Where are my roots? With
Howard Whitman and a black-and-white soda? Or did they
go deep in the Faubourg St. Germain des Pres? Shall I put
them down in Chicago? I met some charming people from
San Francisco, last summer. They say once you've lived in
San Francisco, you're spoiled for the rest of America. But
then I begin to wonder: once you've lived in Paris, are you
spoiled for the rest of the world? I wouldn't like that to hap-

pen. I'm willing to shop around. (*She sees something inside the house*) Do you know? I have an evening dress very much like that . . . (*She is pointing to the interior and craning her neck*) My little couturier stole it from Dior. No, mine's twice as smart.

FAIRCHILD

I have some money put away for you, that I was going to give you when you'd settled down. But you can have it now.

SABRINA

(*Protesting with a smile*)
Oh, Father! I'm a self-supporting woman!

FAIRCHILD

I'd like to give it to you now.

SABRINA

Thank you, Father.

FAIRCHILD

You don't ever have to worry about money.

SABRINA

I love you for many things, Father, but do you know what I love you for most of all? (*He waits for her to go on*) That you decided to become a chauffeur because you wanted to have time to read. (*She smiles at him brightly, with deep fondness*) And all my life I've pictured you, in that long succession of Cadillacs, with the good light you'd rigged over the driver's seat, waiting for the Larrabees, and reading. Through the twenties, the thirties, the forties; in rain and snow and hail and sleet, not caring if it was Aristotle or Anthony Hope, so long as it gave you black words on white paper to feed on. How many books is it now, father?

FAIRCHILD

Six thousand, three hundred and twenty-eight.

SABRINA

(*Grinning*)

I am the daughter of a literary tapeworm.
    (*Pause.*)

FAIRCHILD

Sabrina, I like you.

SABRINA

Thank you, Father. I want you to.

FAIRCHILD

Won't you come home?

SABRINA

(*Rising*)

All right. What's that you're reading now?

FAIRCHILD

Lucretius: *The Nature Of The Universe.*

SABRINA

Oh, yes. That was required reading in our sophomore year.
Much too deep for me. Do you understand it?

FAIRCHILD

No, but I enjoy reading it.

SABRINA

That's fair enough.
    (*They go off toward the garage.*)

FAIRCHILD

(*As they go:*)

I've liked my life, Sabrina.

SABRINA

I know. And I'm glad.

(LINUS *comes out from behind the archway and watches them go, thoughtfully. The bar door opens, and* JULIA *appears.*)

JULIA

Ah! Home is the hunter. Or is it the sailor? You've been missed. We were about to beat the bushes for you.

LINUS

You overrate me, Aunt Julia. I've got too old for that sort of thing.

JULIA

I've always thought that sort of thing was overrated, anyway.

(DAVID *appears from the house.*)

DAVID

Linus, I have come with a message. Our mother is displeased with you.

LINUS

I am displeased with our mother.

DAVID

(*Amused*)

For the same reason? Mary Townsend? (LINUS *nods*) You know, in a way this party is for Mary. And for you. Mother has decided Mary is the girl to housebreak you.

LINUS

Mother is wrong.

DAVID

Well, don't take it out on Mary.

LINUS

I have been a devoted partner and a dutiful son. I have dined with Mary, drunk with Mary, and danced with Mary. What more would they have me do with Mary?

JULIA

Your mother worries about you, Linus.

LINUS

I'm sorry for that.

JULIA

And she's begun to wonder at what point an eligible young bachelor becomes a lecherous old bachelor. Have you any views on the subject?

LINUS

I haven't given it much thought. But I'll be glad to ask among my lecherous old friends.

JULIA

You don't think Mary Townsend's the one to save you from that dread fate.

LINUS

No.

DAVID

Mary's a fine girl, Linus.

LINUS

Mary *is* a fine girl. That's why Mother shouldn't do this to her.

DAVID

Ah, but Mary likes it. And Mary's mother likes it. And Mary's father thinks you're very sound. Very sound indeed.

LINUS

Mary's father is an ass.

JULIA

Agreed.

DAVID

He's made a lot of money.

LINUS

I know a lot of asses who've made a lot of money. Benjamin Townsend is that particular kind of an ass who thinks making money is a holy rite of which he is the anointed high priest. If he should ever discover it's a small knack, like juggling three oranges, he'd fall apart. (*He almost growls*) If making money were all there was to business, it would hardly be worth going to the office once a week. Money's a by-product.

DAVID

But such an attractive by-product.

JULIA

(*Staring at* LINUS *thoughtfully*)
What's the main object in view, Linus? Power?

LINUS

(*After a moment*)

That's become a dirty word.

JULIA

Most of the strong words have.
(*He meets her challenging gaze steadfastly. Finally:*)

LINUS

Control.
(*She nods.*)

DAVID

Well, you've got quite a bit of that. You are Larrabee Industries. Still, marrying Mary would give you a bit more.
There's Townsend Steel and Townsend Sulphur . . .

JULIA

The bride wore a satin gown edged with old common and
preferred stock, and carried a bouquet of debentures.

LINUS

(*Lightly, but deeply serious underneath*)

If I should ever decide I wanted control of Townsend
Steel and Townsend Sulphur, I'd like to think I could get
it without prostituting the Townsend daughter.

DAVID

That's a noble thought.

LINUS

Or myself.

JULIA

That's an afterthought. Be careful of those better instincts, Linus. They don't go with your reputation. (*She moves to the house*) Shall I check you in?

LINUS

I'd rather you didn't.

JULIA

You're still in the bushes. (*A moment*) Linus? (*He looks at her*) If I were thirty years younger, you wouldn't have a chance.

LINUS

I wouldn't put up a struggle.
> (*She raises her glass to him, and goes in.*)

DAVID

You'd better come along in.

LINUS

Not yet.

DAVID

I'll protect you.

LINUS

It's time we stirred things up, David. Serenity can be damned dull.

DAVID

Not for me. The quiet life for me.
> (*A* YOUNG MAN *and a* YOUNG LADY *have eased out of the house rather carefully, and now work above them and make a break for the gardens.* LINUS *catches sight of them.*)

LINUS

Hello!
(*They stop short.*)

THE YOUNG MAN

Oh, hello, Linus, David. Going in to supper?

LINUS

Is it worth it?

THE YOUNG MAN

Yes, it's quite a spread. Betty has a headache. We thought
we'd stroll down to the boathouse. Get some air.

LINUS

You'll find the boathouse pretty cold.

THE YOUNG WOMAN

We weren't going to stay there!

LINUS

Have you ever seen mother's rose garden? It's quite beautiful in the moonlight. It's on the second terrace down, with
a stone fountain, and a little house at the end we call "The
Hideaway."
(*Pause.*)

THE YOUNG WOMAN

I like roses.

THE YOUNG MAN

Yes, that sounds nice. We'll take a look. Thanks, Linus.
(*They start off quite casually.*)

75

LINUS

Glad to be of assistance.
(*They glance over their shoulders once, then disappear.*)

DAVID

What was that for?

LINUS

A small experiment in traffic management. Shouldn't you be doing that sort of thing?

DAVID

(*Grinning*)
Give me time. The evening's young.

LINUS

You're not doing yourself any good out here.

DAVID

Okay. (*But he doesn't move, and then after a moment's hesitation:*) Linus . . . what's become of my dear ex-wife, Gretchen?
(LINUS *turns his head and looks at him reflectively.*)

LINUS

You didn't like that, did you?

DAVID

It wasn't the best joke in the world.

LINUS

I'm sorry. It seemed funny at the time. But the joke wore thin.

DAVID

Do you still see her?

LINUS

(*Shaking his head*)
We came to an understanding. That we had no understanding.

DAVID

Good enough. She had it coming.
(*And then he looks up and smiles apologetically for
having said it.*)

LINUS

And still you miss being married, don't you?

DAVID

I never was married, really. But I'd like to be. I miss being in love.

LINUS

Such a drain on the resources, David. It leaves so little time
for anything else.

DAVID

Are you sure the things you occupy yourself with are that
much more important? I'd like to prove to myself that marriage can be a pretty good occupation.

LINUS

(*With an approving smile*)
Then we'll have to put you to work. Go find yourself a girl.

DAVID

Okay. (*He moves toward the door*) Will you come in soon?
(LINUS *nods*) *Make* it soon, will you?

77

(He raises his hand in a small, affectionate farewell, and goes in.

Long pause.

LINUS *wanders up the terrace, is about to light a cigarette when he sees someone coming from the garage. He flicks out the match and steps into shadow.* SABRINA *appears, takes her sweater from the wall where she left it, glances at the house and turns back toward the garage.)*

LINUS

Hello, Sabrina.
(She turns back.)

SABRINA

Oh, hello.
(And at that moment, the female member of the first amorous couple we saw comes stalking through the opening in the garden wall and heads for the house grimly. She is followed in a moment by her confused and slightly disheveled young man, who is trying to fix his tie as he hurries after her. No sooner have they disappeared into the house, when the girl of the second couple appears from the garden and heads for the bar. Her young man is right behind her, and still eager.)

THE YOUNG MAN

But it's all right! They're gone!

THE YOUNG WOMAN

Oh, shut up!
(They go into the bar.)

SABRINA

My, they looked mad, didn't they?

LINUS

Yes, I wonder why.

SABRINA

(*Amused*)
Where do you suppose they'd been? At "The Hideaway?"

LINUS

I imagine so. Ever been there?

SABRINA

Oh, yes. But never at night. And never . . . (*And with that "And never," she comes back to where she'd been, and assumes a quiet formality. He waits. Then she speaks matter-of-factly, with no sense of apology or self-consciousness*) I came out for a breath of air.

LINUS

So did I.
(*Pause.*)

SABRINA

Good night.

LINUS

Good night. (*She turns and goes. He watches until she is well across. Then:*) Do you still have a scar on your right leg? (*She stops and turns and stares at him, startled.*)

SABRINA

Yes.

LINUS

(*Nods dismissal*)

Good night.

SABRINA

Good night. (*She turns again and goes off. He waits. She reappears*) How did you know about that scar on my leg?

LINUS

I put it there.

SABRINA

When?

LINUS

A long time ago. I came running across there from around back of the garage, and didn't see you, and knocked you crashing into that trellis. You don't remember.

SABRINA

No.

LINUS

You were a very little girl. I picked you up and set you there on the wall, and tried to get you to stop crying. But you wouldn't stop. And when I set you down, you ran away.

SABRINA

Oh. (*She considers, then smiles*) I think that deep Freudian wound should have healed by now.

LINUS

I hope so. I washed the other one off with cold water.

SABRINA

Thank you. (*Pause*) I'm sorry I hit you in the stomach with the hat box.

LINUS

It was rather familiar.

SABRINA

Well, for someone who knows where that scar is because he put it there . . . Still, we never did know each other, did we?

LINUS

And there's not much we can do about it, at this distance.

SABRINA

No. (*She comes to him slowly and stands before him*) Ten years difference in age is a large gap, isn't it?

LINUS

Only among children.

SABRINA

What would you like to know?

LINUS

How you like being home.

SABRINA

It's . . . interesting.

LINUS

And what you've done these past two weeks.

81

SABRINA

Wandered about New York, mostly. I don't really know New York. That's been fun.

LINUS

You should have called me when you were in town. I'd have taken you to lunch.

SABRINA

I hardly know you. (*He acknowledges that one*) But David's taken me to lunch. He's been sweet.

LINUS

And how you liked Paris.

SABRINA

Very much. Oh, very much.

LINUS

Was the job interesting?

SABRINA

Yes. Especially towards the end.

LINUS

Were you good at it?

SABRINA

I was very good at it. I went from file clerk to secretary to private secretary, and ended with a secretary of my own. I was quick, bright, and efficient.

LINUS

Sterling qualities in a woman.

SABRINA

Oh?

LINUS

But I can see you have others.

SABRINA

It sounds as though you were interviewing me for a job.

LINUS

Maybe I am.

SABRINA

Thank you, I'm not looking for a job.

LINUS

Who were you private secretary to?

SABRINA

(*Reciting, with a smile*)

Assistant Economic Commissioner Office of Special Representative for Europe Economic Cooperation Administration. Paris.

LINUS

France?

SABRINA

For security reasons we cannot give out that information.
(*They grin at each other.*)

83

LINUS

Will you do something for me?

SABRINA

What?
(*He takes her by the elbow and conducts her to the wall. There, he turns her and puts his hands under her elbows.*)

LINUS

Up!!
(*He lifts her to a seat on the wall.*)

SABRINA

(*Smiling*)
I may burst out crying again.

LINUS

That's what I want to see.

SABRINA

(*With a look of surprise*)
I almost could! I wonder why?

LINUS

You're still a little girl. (*A moment, then:*) How did you get your name?

SABRINA

Sabrina? From father's reading, of course. He was struggling through Milton's "Comus" when I was born; "The Masque of Comus."
(*She quotes*)
"Sabrina Fair
Listen where thou art sitting

Under the glassy, cool, translucent wave
In twisted braids of lilies knitting
The loose train of thy amber-dropping hair."
Poor father. He got fooled.

LINUS

And what does it mean?

SABRINA

In one sentence, so that he who does not wish to read may
run, it is the story of a water nymph who saves a virgin from
a fate worse than death.

LINUS

Is Sabrina the virgin?

SABRINA

(Coldly, precisely)
Sabrina is the savior.
(Pause.)

LINUS

(Abruptly)
Why did you run away from Paris?

SABRINA

(Ruefully)
That was a good guess. I don't see how a thing like that
could show.

LINUS

Was it because you were in love with him, or because you
weren't?

SABRINA

Are you always so . . . perceptive?

85

LINUS

Only in business dealings.

SABRINA

Is this business?

LINUS

You may have something I want.

SABRINA

I hardly think so. Good night.
> (*She braces with her hands to spring down from the wall, but he stops her.*)

LINUS

You're too little a girl to jump to such big conclusions. Is he French or is he American, and did you run away because he wants to marry you or because he doesn't?

SABRINA

(*Her eyes narrow, and she speaks in cold anger, precisely*)
He is French. He wishes to marry me. You are being presumptuous in a way you wouldn't be with anyone else, and I don't like it. Good night. (*She gives him a sharp push away and jumps down and starts for the garage. Unfortunately, however, having had the last word, she can't help adding another over her shoulder*) And he's extremely rich!

LINUS

(*Delighted*)
Why, you little snob!
> (SABRINA *stops and turns, amazed.*)

SABRINA

(*Outraged*)

Me! ? !

LINUS

Yes, you! Did you think you could impress me with the fact that a rich Frenchman wants to marry you? How rich is he? Is he richer than I am?

SABRINA

(*Sadly*)

Oh. I didn't mean it that way.

LINUS

Yes, you did. And quite right, too. The rich are impressed by money; they have to be.

SABRINA

You're not.

LINUS

Some are contemptuous of money; they can afford to be. Will you come back to your wall?

SABRINA

No.

LINUS

You may as well tell me about it. You have no one else to tell.

SABRINA

That's not true! (*Then, considering*) Yes, it is.

LINUS

Besides, it's sometimes better to tell these things to . . . a
stranger.

(*And at this she must smile broadly, and he takes ad-
vantage of the smile to move to her and take her
firmly by the elbows and set her up on a nearby table.*)

SABRINA

(*Very much the little girl, wailing*)
Why do I have to perch?

LINUS

It lets me feel that I have you.

SABRINA

I don't want you to feel that you have me!

LINUS

You must tell me everything, my child.

SABRINA

I don't like the sound of that, either! Why isn't there any
music?

LINUS

They've gone in to supper. Would you like a drink?

SABRINA

Yes!

LINUS

I'll get you one in a minute. Is he madly in love with you?

SABRINA

Yes!

88

LINUS

Are you madly in love with him?

SABRINA

No! But I'm madly in love with the life he offers. And that's the trouble.

LINUS

Loads of money and a house in Paris.

SABRINA

And a house in Burgundy, with a vineyard! A *real* vineyard that makes one of the very *best* burgundies!

LINUS

That *is* an attraction! And a good Burgundian cook to go with it?

SABRINA

Oh, a fantastic cook! I can't tell you! The most amazing food you've ever tasted!

LINUS

You must ask me down. What else?

SABRINA

The south of France when it's gay, and London once a year; and skiing at Chamonix, or in Switzerland at Davos, or in Austria—there's a little place in Austria he says has the best skiing in Europe but I forget the name—and oh! shooting! He loves to shoot and he's a wonderful shot, and the woods are so lovely in autumn. (*Like a little girl showing off, proudly*) Wild boar.

89

LINUS
(*Fascinated*)

Eh?

SABRINA
(*Proudly*)
He shoots wild boar in Belgium.

LINUS

I'll marry him myself.
(*Which breaks it for* SABRINA, *and she laughs aloud.*)

SABRINA

Don't be fooled; he's not a playboy. He works hard.

LINUS

At what?

SABRINA

Stocks and bonds and industries and things. You know—
deals. He goes to Switzerland a lot.

LINUS

On skis?

SABRINA

Oh, really!

LINUS

What's his name?

SABRINA

I won't tell you.

LINUS

I think you've made him up.

SABRINA

I have not! He's five-feet-eleven and weighs a hundred-and-sixty pounds and wears glasses, and has a lovely moustache.

LINUS

Sounds like the entire French Chamber of Deputies.

SABRINA

He's a very distinguished person!

LINUS

He offers you a great deal, Sabrina.

SABRINA

(*Softly, glowing*)

I know. The house in Paris is lovely . . . and all the things that go with it; the people and the places; the clothes and the jewels . . . (*She chuckles softly*) I would even have a car and chauffeur of my own.

LINUS

Is that your own private little joke, or does he share it?

(*Her eyes narrow a little, and she smiles frostily.*)

SABRINA

He calls me—"*sa petite fille du chauffeur,*" which, in your schoolboy French, may be translated as: "his little daughter of the chauffeur."

LINUS

A term of endearment, I take it, like—"my little cabbage."

91

SABRINA

Exactly.

LINUS

I apologize.

SABRINA

You should.

LINUS

Why don't you marry him?
(*Pause.*)

SABRINA

I'm afraid.

LINUS

Of what?

SABRINA

Of being domesticated. (*He laughs*) That's not funny. Do you think men have the exclusive right to run from domestication? Pooh! That's a myth! Men adore it!

LINUS

You've found that out.

SABRINA

Yes.

LINUS

And you want no part of domesticity.

SABRINA

I didn't say that. I love being domestic. I'm afraid of being domesticated. There's a difference.

LINUS

(*Impressed*)

Ah, you've found that out, too.

SABRINA

Do you understand that?

LINUS

(*Almost grimly*)

Yes. I do.

SABRINA

The trouble with marriage is that men want to give you the world, but it has to be the world they want to give you. And what of the other worlds outside the window? Do you know what I mean? The things he does are fun to do, and I love doing them with him, and you can't have a marriage without that. But suppose then I find that they keep me from doing all the other wonderful things I've wanted to do? Suppose I find that instead of opening up my life, I've closed it down and locked it off?

LINUS

You can't do everything, Sabrina.

SABRINA

Ah, but it's important to try! And if marrying him should keep me from trying, then the most terrible thing in the world would happen. I'd get bored.

LINUS

Is that the most terrible thing in the world?

SABRINA

To be bored? Oh, yes! Are you ever bored?

LINUS
(*Promptly, mockingly*)

Never!

SABRINA

Oh, that's *good!*
(*And she stares at him with encouraging approval.
He, in turn, stares back in exasperated amusement.*)

LINUS

What do you want to do, Sabrina?

SABRINA

Everything.

LINUS

What *can* you do?

SABRINA
(*A bit ruefully*)

Nothing impressive. (*Musically, thinking aloud*) I cannot
sing a song or write a poem or paint a picture, and I shall
never run for Senator from Connecticut . . .

LINUS

Why Connecticut?

SABRINA

It makes a nice sound.

LINUS

Oh?

SABRINA

But I think I have a talent, all the same. I think I have a
talent for living. Perhaps I'm trying to make the most of

94

something small for want of something better, but I think a true talent for living has the quality of creation, and if that's the talent I was meant to have, I'm awfully glad I have it. I'd rather live a first-rate life than paint a second-rate picture.

(LINUS *is gently amused at this self-dramatization.*)

LINUS

So would a lot of second-rate painters. Do you know how to live a first-rate life?

SABRINA

I'm beginning to learn; I've been to school.

LINUS

In Paris. (*She nods*) And what did Paris teach you?

SABRINA

(*Proudly*)

Two things! To develop my appetites; and to discipline them.

LINUS

That's admirable.

SABRINA

And to want to do everything and see everything, sense everything and feel everything and taste everything; to know that life is an enormous experience and must be used. To be in the world, and of the world, and never to stand aside and watch.

LINUS

You never learned that in Paris.

SABRINA

Where, then?

LINUS

It sounds more like Ralph Waldo Emerson.

SABRINA

You mustn't laugh at me.

LINUS

I could hardly laugh at such an impressive mixture of high principles and higher living. Sabrina, how would you like to be a Joan of Arc, and march at the head of a devout company of transcendental epicureans, who shall find happiness in doing, grace in skiing at Chamonix, and conquer the world with a cook book? Whose aim shall be: a bottle of the very best burgundy on every table; a tin of pâté de foie gras on every shelf? And whose motto, inscribed on the banner you carry, shall be . . .

SABRINA

What?

LINUS

What else? "Let them eat cake!"

SABRINA

(*Laughing*)

I like that! But you are laughing at me, and you shouldn't.

LINUS

I can't help it. You have another talent, Sabrina: a talent for making me laugh. Paris has gone to your head, Sabrina. You've learned too much too fast, and your worldliness is a little soft around the edges.

SABRINA

Oh. The day I came home. (*She winces slightly, thinking of it*) The cockatoo was not a success, was it? (*He shakes his head*) It seemed such a nice idea at the time.

LINUS

It was a romantic idea, as most of your ideas seem to be. Shall I teach you to be realistic?

SABRINA

Do you think you can?

LINUS
(*Deadly serious*)

In one easy lesson. Marry your Frenchman. You'll never have it so good again. (*She stares at him anxiously*) Have no qualms, Sabrina. Marrying for love is a romantic American idea.

SABRINA
(*Hopefully*)

I'm fond of him.

LINUS

Do you love someone else?

SABRINA

I'm not sure. There's someone I think I've been in love with all my life, but since it goes way back, it may not be real, now. I've never had a chance to find out.

LINUS

Don't bother to find out. Marry your Frenchman.

SABRINA

Oh, no! I must find out!

LINUS

Would it do you any good if you did?

SABRINA

I don't think so.

LINUS

Then don't bother.

SABRINA

That's not the kind of advice you give yourself. You seem to be spending your life finding out.

LINUS

We're looking for different things. I've shot wild boar in Belgium.

SABRINA
(*Delighted*)

You have?

LINUS

Marry your Frenchman, Sabrina. Don't compare yourself to me. I've already got a chauffeur.

SABRINA

That was unkind.

LINUS
(*Grimly*)

How to be realistic in one easy lesson.

SABRINA

I want to find out!

LINUS

Who is this you think you're in love with?
(DAVID *appears from the house.*)

DAVID

Hey, Linus!

SABRINA

(*Startled*)

Oh!

LINUS

(*Just as startled, when he sees her reaction*)
David? Is it David?

SABRINA

(*In confusion*)

Ah!
(DAVID *has run down the steps and crossed to them.*)

DAVID

(*Grimly, to* LINUS)
Now you *are* being rude.

LINUS

Oh. Mary. Yes, I guess I am. (*He is tense with delight and excitement*) Sabrina wants a drink. I was just about to get it for her.

DAVID

I'll get it. What would you like, Sabrina?

SABRINA

Scotch, please. With soda, lots of soda.
(DAVID *starts for the bar.* LINUS *stops to move a chair.*)

LINUS

What's Mary doing?

DAVID

Sitting in the living room with Harry Selby, explaining how they make steel.

(DAVID *goes into the bar. As soon as he is gone,* LINUS *speeds back to* SABRINA *and leans across to her with eager delight.*)

LINUS

It *is* David, isn't it?

SABRINA

(*Defiantly*)

No!

LINUS

It has to be! Someone you've known all your life! It couldn't be anyone else!

SABRINA

Just because I was brought up there over the garage doesn't mean I was cloistered!

LINUS

Don't tell me it's Howard Whitman who went to school with you and now jerks sodas in Oyster Bay?

SABRINA

How did you know about *him?*

LINUS

You have no secrets from me, Sabrina.

SABRINA

It might be someone I met at college!

LINUS

You went to a women's college!

SABRINA

We sometimes imported men!

LINUS

Sabrina, be honest! It's David! Do you want him? You can have him!

SABRINA

Don't say that!

LINUS

Why not? (*He is in a fever of intense delight*) Oh, this is better than the Frenchman! You've developed expensive tastes in men, Sabrina. But David's the one to give you the world. Even the most bountiful of Frenchmen are careful. Take David, Sabrina. David's the one!

SABRINA

(*Frightened*)
You make it sound like a game!

LINUS

(*Savagely*)
It is a game! The most exciting game in the world! With life-size figures! Who shall capture whom, and who shall capture the world!

SABRINA

What about love?

LINUS

(*With contemptuous assurance*)
What *about* love? Love is the measure of defeat. The one who loves is captured.

SABRINA

(*Unequal to this struggle*)
Ah, no!

LINUS

Must you have it with love? Then remember, Sabrina, you left someone behind in Paris and came three thousand miles because you've loved David all your life!

SABRINA

No, to find out!

LINUS

And you'd be so good for David! You're what David needs! All you have to do is tell him you've always loved him . . . and he'll fall like a peach. Think of it, Sabrina! All your dreams come true, and twice over! Two men, and yours for the taking *You* have the power of choice! You! "*La petite fille du chauffeur*" . . . *you* are in the driver's seat! (*And with that, he thinks he hears* DAVID *coming, and races across and up the steps and stops in the doorway of the house to face across to* SABRINA. *The bar door opens, and* DAVID *appears, holding two highballs.* LINUS *raises an admonishing finger*) Take him!

(*He runs into the house.* SABRINA *stares after him, rigid with anxiety.*)

The Curtain Falls

ACT THREE

ACT THREE

The following morning MARGARET, *the maid, is clearing breakfast dishes from a table in the walled garden and is placing them on a tray. It is late in the morning; the sun is high.* LINUS *appears on the terrace in the same old sailing clothes he wore when we first met him. He wanders to the edge of the terrace. He carries a small leather volume of verse.*

LINUS

Margaret, have you seen Mr. David?

MARGARET

It's his breakfast dishes I'm clearing away, sir. And that late, he'll not eat a bite of lunch.

LINUS

Where's he gone?

MARGARET

He's walking in the garden with your mother.
(*He glances to the north, but does not see them. He walks down the steps, then stops, irresolutely. He looks off to the garage, sees nothing, and turns his attention to the transfer of plates from table to tray.*)

LINUS

(*After a while*)
I don't suppose you've seen Sabrina this morning.

MARGARET

Sabrina? Yes, sir. She's up there on the balcony, sunning herself.

(LINUS, *surprised, looks over at the garage, sees something, and is puzzled.*)

LINUS

Where's her face?

MARGARET

(*Amused*)

It's her hair that's covering it, sir: she's drying her hair.

(*He nods, accepting the explanation as rational, and moves across to call.*)

LINUS

(*Calling*)

Sabrina?

SABRINA

(*From off stage*)

What? Oh! Good morning, Linus! (*Her voice is bright and gay*) I thought of something last night, much later, and I've been saving it for you! If I'm Joan of Arc, then you must be Alexander the Great! (*He winces and glances at* MARGARET, *who has stopped work at this. He looks back to* SABRINA, *who takes that as her cue to explain*) Weeping for new worlds to conquer!

(*He winces again, terribly.*)

LINUS

Come down here. I want to talk to you.

SABRINA

What?

LINUS

Come down here!

SABRINA

I can't! I've just washed my hair!

LINUS

That doesn't matter.

SABRINA

Yes, it does! When a girl washes her hair, she takes off all her clothes! At least, I do!

LINUS

I want to talk to you!

SABRINA

What about? (*He makes no answer*) Is someone there? Oh! Margaret, you mustn't listen! This is a private conversation!

MARGARET

(*Bristling with indignation*)

I'm sure I have no interest in anything you have to say, young lady.

(*And with great bustle, she moves the tray and scrubs the table.*)

SABRINA

Isn't it a beautiful morning, Linus? The minute I woke up and looked out the window, I knew I would have to wash my hair!

LINUS

(Imperatively)

Sabrina!

SABRINA

(With mocking gaiety)

Yes, Linus! I found out!

(He makes a move in her direction, but stops short as he sees her go into her room. We hear the screen door slam. He stares after her in exasperated amusement. JULIA *appears on the terrace, carrying a cup of coffee.)*

LINUS

She seems happy, Margaret.

MARGARET

She was always a happy child, sir.

(She picks up the tray and starts for the house.)

LINUS

Bring me some coffee, will you please?

MARGARET

Yes, sir.

(She goes into the house.)

JULIA

(Sitting down, shakily)

I'll be honest: I have a teentsy-weentsy hangover. From one half, of one glass, of champagne. *(She quotes, with some distaste)* "Grow old along with me . . . The best is yet to be . . ." Robert Browning was a damned fool.

LINUS

Aunt Julia . . .

JULIA

Hmmm?

LINUS

A young lady awakens in the morning, looks out the window, and decides to wash her hair. What does it mean?

JULIA

Linus, I'm not up to playing games this morning.

LINUS

Would it mean that something particularly nice has happened to her?

JULIA

It quite often does. More often, it means that her hair needs washing. Anybody I know?

LINUS

(*Turning away*)

When are you going to let me take you sailing, Aunt Julia?

JULIA

I could never see the charm in getting wet at a forty-five degree angle. You're looking terribly pleased with yourself, this morning.

LINUS

Yes, I feel quite godlike this morning.

JULIA

There's no use asking why.

LINUS

Not at this point in the game.

JULIA

What game?

LINUS

Have you ever shot wild boar in Belgium, Aunt Julia? (*She winces; her head does ache*) We must have David take it up.

JULIA

Linus, there are times when your way of saying and doing the unexpected has a certain charm. But not this morning.

LINUS

(*Cheerfully*)

My only pleasure in life is doing the unexpected. It has made me greatly admired in business, and greatly frowned on in society.

(JULIA *opens her eyes and fixes him with a direct look.*)

JULIA

I think you thought that up, one day, and wrote it down.

LINUS

(*Grinning*)

Why, Aunt Julia!

(MAUDE *and* DAVID *appear from the garden, deep in conversation.* MAUDE *looks exasperated;* DAVID *has a set smile.*)

DAVID

. . . After all, I'm not a child.

MAUDE

No, David, I *am* surprised at your attitude. There's no earthly reason why you should have a chip on your shoulder.

DAVID

Obviously I'm going to have trouble with my family.

MAUDE

Not at all! But you certainly owe it to us to sit down and discuss the matter quietly. . . . (*She becomes aware of* LINUS *and* JULIA) Oh.

LINUS

What happened to you last night, David? You suddenly disappeared.

DAVID

(*Pleased with himself*)

I went sailing.

LINUS

At midnight?

DAVID

There was a wonderful, lopsided moon. . . .

LINUS

Yes, there was, wasn't there? But I don't remember that there was anyone at the party worth sharing it with.

DAVID

There wasn't. At the party.

MAUDE

Linus: David wants to marry Sabrina. You know . . . (*She waves at the garage.* LINUS *sucks in his breath, and his eyes widen with suppressed pleasure and triumph.* JULIA

111

stares at him) Julia, we've agreed not to say anything for a while . . .

DAVID
(*Impatiently*)

Now, Mother!

MAUDE

Well, Linus?
(LINUS *exhales, and grins at* DAVID.)

LINUS

Congratulations.

MAUDE

Oh.

DAVID
(*Gratefully*)

Thank you, Linus.

MAUDE

There! You see, David? No one in the family is going to be against you. We can all understand your falling in love with the girl. But are you sure you want to marry her?

DAVID

Mother, we've been through all that. And I resent your putting Sabrina in the category of . . .

MAUDE

I'm not putting her in any category, David. I'm very fond of the girl, but . . .

LINUS

Mother, if you don't mind, I'd like to know how it happened. What's the story, David?

DAVID

You were here. Remember? I brought her a drink, and we talked for a while, and then we decided to go out on the water. We didn't sail; I took the cruiser. The wind was dropping and I was afraid of the tide. (LINUS *nods agreement*) And that's all. We wandered about the Sound all night, and talked.

MAUDE

That's exactly what I mean. How can you know you want to marry a girl, after spending one night out on the Sound talking to her?

LINUS

What would you have suggested he do with her? (*His mother fixes him icily*) Sorry, Mother.

DAVID

(*With a regretful smile*)
As to that, I tried that, too, but she wouldn't let me.

JULIA

Good for her.

MAUDE

Yes, that was clever of her.

JULIA

Ooh!

DAVID

Mother!
(LINUS *gives a sharp whoop of laughter.*)

113

MAUDE

Careful!

(*This last is at sight of* MARGARET, *who appears on the terrace carrying a small silver tray with coffee service for one. They turn and watch her approach and set the tray on the table. But the silence becomes intolerable for* MAUDE, *who was brought up always to fill gaps in the conversation. She speaks up, a bit too brightly*) Margaret, did I tell you to set another place for lunch?

MARGARET

Yes, madam.

MAUDE

Thank you. (MARGARET *pours the coffee, then starts back toward the house.* MAUDE *now has something to talk about*) I had the most amusing conversation on the phone yesterday afternoon. It was a man calling from New York to say he had just arrived from Paris and was stopping at the St. Regis and had a note of introduction to me from Madge de Lessac, and could he deliver it in person. He sounded so charming, I took a chance and asked him out to lunch. I'm sure Madge wouldn't send me anyone who . . . (MARGARET *is gone.*) Now, David! I don't want to continue this discussion until after I've talked to your father. But I want you to believe something. Will you? I want you to believe that I am on your side. (*And now, at her most wide-eyed*) Oh, how could you even dream that I would be against anything you wanted, unless I thought it was wrong for you? You remember, dear, I was never very happy about Gretchen.

DAVID

(*Uncomfortably*)

Yes, Mother, I remember. And this is different.

MAUDE

Of course it's different! (*And then*) Are you sure it's different, David?

DAVID

Yes.

MAUDE

(*Softly*)

You wanted Gretchen just as much. It may not be different, David.

DAVID

Yes, this girl is different from any girl I've ever known. (*To* LINUS) You remember what I said to you last night. (LINUS *nods*) There she was, all the time. It didn't take long to find out. When you're with her, you find yourself suddenly talking about things you've always wanted to do that you've forgotten. You become aware of all the things you've missed and all the things you're missing. She's so much in love with life, there's so much of the feeling of life in her, that you want to take hold, you want to have her, because maybe if you do, you'll have what she has. I know it sounds . . . young. But when you're with her, that's how you feel.

MAUDE

(*Softly, smiling, almost weeping for his innocence*)

Ah, David . . . don't you know that if there were anyone like that in the world, I would turn the world over to get her for you?

DAVID

There she is, Mother.

MAUDE

You're my sweet, idiot child. Linus, will you tell him?

LINUS

(*Stolidly*)

Tell him what, Mother?

(*She stares at him, then at* DAVID, *and decides she can say no more.*)

MAUDE

Very well, I'll talk to your father. He's gone to a funeral; he should be in a good humor. And no matter what happens, I expect all of you to be full of bright chitchat at lunch. *Damn* Madge de Lessac! *I* would never plop someone down on *her* out of a clear sky and say, "Have him for lunch." Oh! Fairchild. (FAIRCHILD *has appeared at left*) Is the funeral over? Already?

FAIRCHILD

Yes, madam. Jessie said you wanted to see me.

MAUDE

No, I . . . oh. Yes, I wanted you to meet someone at the station, but I decided you wouldn't be back in time, so I sent John. (*She stares at him, thinking there should be something more to say, then gives up*) Thank you, Fairchild.

(*He nods and goes. She stares after him. Pause.*)

DAVID

(*With a small smile*)

I know what you're thinking, Mother.

MAUDE
(*Coldly*)

He's a very sweet man. And very well read. Go find your father. (DAVID *starts for the house*) And David. Not a word.

DAVID

No.
(*He goes.* MAUDE *looks at* LINUS *grimly.*)

MAUDE

Linus, go away.

LINUS

I'd enjoy staying, Mother.

MAUDE

I know you'd enjoy staying. That's why I want you to go.
(*He rises, holding the book of verse, and wanders over in her direction.*)

LINUS

Mother, did you know that Sabrina's name comes from Milton's "The Masque of Comus?" I wonder if David knows this passage. (*He reads*) "Whilst from off the waters fleet / Thus I set my printless feet / Gentle swain, at thy request, I am here."
(*He grins down at his mother.*)

MAUDE

(*Sharply*)

Will you please go.
(*He smiles and starts for the garden.*)

JULIA

Linus, did Sabrina wash her hair this morning?

LINUS

I believe she did, Aunt Julia. I'm thinking of washing mine.

(*He goes.*)

MAUDE

What was that about?

JULIA

I don't know. But I'd like to.

MAUDE

I should have known I was going to have trouble with that girl, the minute she gave me that bird. Ah, my poor, sweet David. A sitting duck if ever there was one.

JULIA

I don't think she's that kind of a girl, Maude.

MAUDE

Don't be silly. Every girl is that kind of a girl. She got a taste of high life in Paris, and decided she'd look for more of it at home. She certainly didn't have to look far. She moved right in with two Cadillacs and a Ford.

JULIA

Maude, I have a feeling about this girl. . . .

MAUDE

And we don't know *any*thing about what she did in Paris!

JULIA

(*Acidly*)

I believe she worked for the United States Government.

MAUDE

You know very well what I mean. No girl moves in the circles she did, and gets to know the people she knew, by being an excellent typist.

(LARRABEE *appears on the terrace.*)

LARRABEE

Good morning, Julia.

JULIA

Good morning. Did you have fun?

LARRABEE

(*To* MAUDE)

David said you wanted to see me.

MAUDE

Yes. (*Hopefully*) Was it a nice funeral, Linus?

LARRABEE

It was a wretched funeral.

MAUDE

Oh.

LARRABEE

People should be horsewhipped for such bungling. It started late, ended early, and from beginning to end, no one seemed to know what he was doing. I never saw such shilly-shallying.

JULIA

But they did get the coffin into the grave.

LARRABEE

Since I was not allowed to attend the interment, I couldn't say. But I'd give two to one against.

MAUDE

Oh, that is too bad. But I suppose the poor things just didn't have time to plan. It *was* an unexpected death, wasn't it?

LARRABEE

How can death be unexpected?
(*He opens a cigarette box, examines the contents, then tries another.*)

JULIA

Maude, do you think a poor, tired old invalid could have her lunch peacefully upstairs on a tray?

MAUDE

Traitor.

JULIA

(*With a sweet smile*)
Thank you.
(*She goes into the house.*)

LARRABEE

Are there no cigarettes of mine out here?

MAUDE

(*Looking in a box he's looked in*)
I'm afraid not, dear.

120

LARRABEE

Never mind.

(*He gets out a pipe and settles himself as* MAUDE *watches.*)

MAUDE

(*Finally*)

We're having a guest for lunch. A friend of Madge de Lessac's, from Paris.

LARRABEE

Is that what you wanted to tell me?

MAUDE

Well, no. I'm sorry you had a bad morning, dear.

LARRABEE

It wasn't completely wasted. They had rather a good hymn that was new to me. I may use it for myself.

MAUDE

That's good.

LARRABEE

I wrote down the number.

(*He begins to hum, trying to remember the tune, but has to give it up as a bad job.*)

MAUDE

Linus . . . David came and talked to me this morning.

LARRABEE

Yes? What about?

MAUDE

He thinks he wants to get married again.

LARRABEE

(In good humor, now)

Resilient, isn't he? Who is it this time? One of those young things he was dancing with last night?

MAUDE

Well, he didn't dance with her. *(Thoughtfully)* I wonder if it was my fault. It may easily have been, now that I think of it. It may never have happened if I had let David ask her to the party. *(She thinks about that.)*

LARRABEE

(After a pause)

Hmmm?

MAUDE

Hell hath no fury like a woman scorned, you know.

LARRABEE

So I've always been given to understand. I doubt if it's been verified. Who is it that was scorned?

MAUDE

Sabrina. We didn't ask her to the party.

LARRABEE

Who's Sabrina?

MAUDE

Sabrina Fairchild. Fairchild's daughter.

LARRABEE

(Remembering)

Oh! Oh, oh, oh! Sabrina! Did she expect to be invited?

MAUDE

Linus, don't you remember? We talked about it.

LARRABEE

Oh, yes.

MAUDE

And I'm sure she wanted to be.

LARRABEE

Well, that's nonsense. But I was quite taken with that girl.
I have a feeling she's going to get somewhere.

MAUDE

She already has.

LARRABEE

Hmmm? Well, let's not get off the subject. Who is it David
wants to marry?

MAUDE

Sabrina.

LARRABEE

Who?

MAUDE
(*Exasperated*)

Oh, Linus, I get so tired of repeating things! Sabrina Fairchild! Your chauffeur's daughter!

LARRABEE
(*After a moment*)

You needn't have put it so bluntly. Where is David?
(*This last almost ominously.*)

MAUDE

Now, Linus, we must discuss this calmly.

LARRABEE

(*With murderous calm*)

I see no reason why it should be discussed at all. (*Calling*)
David!

MAUDE

I'm sory I put it that way; I didn't intend to. The fact that
she's your chauffeur's daughter doesn't really matter, Linus.
People don't care about that sort of thing any more.

LARRABEE

I . . . DO! *David!*

MAUDE

Linus, remember: we're living in the twentieth century!
(*He turns and looks at her as though she had gone
mad, and then speaks with controlled force.*)

LARRABEE

I have lived in the twentieth century for over fifty years,
which is as long as any man has lived in the twentieth century, and longer than most. And I feel I know as much about
it as the next man. Just what has the twentieth century to
do with my son wanting to marry that girl?

MAUDE

Now, gently, Linus. And don't you dare shout at David.

LARRABEE

(*Going on as though he hadn't heard her*)

If the twentieth century encourages that sort of thing,
and that sort of thinking, then it's a damned silly century,

and the sooner we get out of it, the better. (*With quiet loath-ing*) The twentieth century! I could pick a century blind-folded out of a hat and get a better one! (DAVID *appears on the terrace*) Would you mind coming down, please? (DAVID *descends the steps and approaches*) You may go, Maude.

MAUDE
(*With fire*)

I certainly will not go! (LARRABEE *stares at the ground for a long time, and* MAUDE *decides to placate*) Now, dear, this can be done pleasantly, without hurting anyone. . . .

LARRABEE

(*Looks up at* DAVID *and speaks quietly, and quite pleasantly*)

Your mother is concerned for fear I may frighten you by shouting at you. Do you share her concern?

DAVID
No, sir.

LARRABEE

I would be pleased if you would go, Maude. (MAUDE *looks from her son to her husband, makes a moue of resig-nation, and starts for the house. She stops once, as though to say something, then changes her mind and goes*) Can you remember back to the last time I shouted at you?

DAVID
(*After some thought*)

No.

LARRABEE

I will refresh your memory. It was on the Valiant. In the Astor Cup Race. I gave an order to jibe, and you were not paying attention.

DAVID

Oh, yes.

LARRABEE

The boom came over and was about to strike you when I shouted. I shouted to save your life.

DAVID

(*Smiling*)

I don't think it will be necessary again.

LARRABEE

Nor do I. Why do you want to marry this girl?

DAVID

Because I'm in love with her.

LARRABEE

How do you know?

DAVID

I know.

LARRABEE

Have you slept with her?

DAVID

No.

LARRABEE

I am glad to see you have the grace to deny it. (*And he goes on, stopping* DAVID's *abortive protest*) I will say to you what my father said to me when I was younger than you are now. I thought I had said it to you when you were younger, but apparently I was neglectful of my duties. There are two kinds of women in this world: those you sleep with, and those you marry.

DAVID
(Angrily)

I haven't slept with her!

LARRABEE

The first denial is sufficient.

DAVID

Look here, Father . . .

LARRABEE
(Strongly, cutting him off)

No gentleman makes love to a servant in his mother's house!

DAVID

She's not a servant.

LARRABEE

She is a servant's daughter. In behaving as you have, you have not merely betrayed your mother's trust, you have insulted Fairchild, since what you have done is the worst form of condescension. I have too much respect for Fairchild ever to intrude on his personal life; I expect you to have the same respect for his daughter.

DAVID

I have so much respect for his daughter, I want to marry her.

LARRABEE

That's overdoing it. (LINUS *wanders on from the garden*) And just how did you plan to proceed? Will you have Fairchild drive us to church, then change his clothes and escort the bride down the aisle?

DAVID

That wasn't necessary, Father.

LARRABEE

(*To* LINUS)

I suppose you've heard about this proposed . . . alliance.

LINUS

Yes, I have.

LARRABEE

And I suppose you think it's just dandy.

LINUS

Yes, I do. If it's what David wants. And if it's what Sabrina wants.

LARRABEE

(*Abruptly*)

I am coming in to the office on Monday.

LINUS

What for? Nothing you can do can affect David. His money is his own; his share of the company is his own.

LARRABEE

I understand that nothing I can do, or say, can affect my sons. I am coming in to find out why I am being accused of driving young Matthew Loring to the wall.

LINUS

(*His eyes narrowing*)

You haven't driven young Matthew Loring to the wall.

LARRABEE

I know I haven't. But my name also happens to be Linus Larrabee, and people sometimes fall into error and charge me with the sins of my son.

LINUS

(*His eyes alight with the sense of impending battle*)
What sins? What have you heard from your fellow mourners? Anyone can tell you've been to church; you're full of the latest Wall Street gossip.

LARRABEE

Don't make cheap jokes. Matt Loring is one of my oldest friends, and one of the most respected men in New York! What do I say to him the next time I see him?

LINUS

That his son is a thief.

LARRABEE

That's a lie!

LINUS

Don't say that to me. He tried to take a company of mine —to *take* a company—with a trick that would have made Jay Gould blush with shame. What if Matt Loring's a friend of yours? His son's no friend of mine. He tried to move in on me, and I keelhauled him.

LARRABEE

(*Shouting*)
You needn't have spread our name all over the street!

LINUS

I don't give a damn for the good opinion of old men you meet at funerals! When I break a man who tried to break me, I want the world to know it!

LARRABEE

(*Shouting*)

Don't be so damned majestic! Who the hell do you think you are?

(*And on this,* MAUDE *hurries on from the house.*)

MAUDE

Linus! You promised not to shout at David!

LARRABEE

(*Shouting*)

I'm not shouting at David, God damn it!

(*And he falls into a chair, bitter with frustration, but quickly resigned to it.*)

MAUDE

(*To* DAVID)

What is it? What's the matter?

DAVID

(*Disturbed*)

A little business conference.

MAUDE

(*To* LINUS)

I asked you to keep away.

LINUS

I'm sorry. (*To his father*) If you care to come in on Monday, I'll be glad to go over the entire situation with you, and explain exactly what happened.

LARRABEE
(*Quietly*)

I am no longer interested. (*He looks over at* DAVID) Are you sure in your own mind? Do you know what you're doing?

DAVID

Yes.

LARRABEE

And you want to do it.

DAVID

Yes, sir.

LARRABEE
(*With quiet resignation*)

Maude, I will not oppose this marriage. I do not approve of it. I would prevent it if I could. But I will accept it if I have to.

MAUDE

Oh.

(*A long pause, as* LARRABEE *stares off into space, moodily. Then, finally, he glances over at* DAVID.)

LARRABEE

This sort of thing wouldn't have happened if you'd gone to Harvard.

(MARGARET *appears on the terrace.*)

MAUDE

Yes, Margaret.

MARGARET

The guest has arrived, madam. Mr. Paul d'Ar . . . (*She consults the calling card*) . . . d'Ar . . .

MAUDE

D'Argenson, Margaret. Yes. Will you bring Monsieur . . . (*She enunciates meticulously, as to a child*) —d'Ar-gen-son to us here, please. (MARGARET *goes.* MAUDE *turns to her family*) Now, we'll have no more talk about it. I'll speak to Fairchild the first chance I get. But if this man knows Madge de Lessac, he probably knows other friends of ours. While he is here, I want no mention of Sabrina, and I don't want to hear the word "marriage." I am quite fed up with marriage and consider it a deplorable institution. (*And then, with great charm*) Ah, Monsieur d'Argenson!

> (*This, of course, to the guest, who is ushered on to the terrace by* MARGARET, *who then retires.* PAUL D'ARGENSON *is five-foot-eleven, weighs a hundred-and-sixty pounds, has a lovely moustache, and wears glasses. He is a year or two younger than* LINUS, *and gives the immediate impression of being an affable and good-natured man. He wears a permanent smile that crinkles his eyes behind the heavy, black-rimmed, peculiarly French glasses, and gives that part of his face a slightly Japanese cast. The eyes are alive and perceptive. With his affability, the man has authority. He wears a dark business suit. He crosses the terrace as he speaks, and his accent is rather startling to an American, for it has an overlay of Oxonian English.*)

PAUL

Mrs. Larrabee, how good of you to ask me out. (*They shake hands*) I do hope you forgive me for calling you on the telephone.

MAUDE

But I was delighted! How dull it would have been to mail the letter and miss the week-end!

PAUL

I am here only a short time, you see, and I have heard so much about you from . . . oh, the letter!
(*He produces it from a pocket.*)

MAUDE

It was sweet of Madge to send you to me. (*She pockets the letter*) This is my husband. Linus—Monsieur Paul d'Argenson.

LARRABEE

How do you do.
(*They shake hands.*)

PAUL

Mr. Larrabee . . .

MAUDE

My son Linus,—my son David . . .
(*They shake hands.*)

LINUS

Hello . . .

DAVID

Nice to see you.

PAUL

I am most charmed to meet you all. And may I say that it is an imposingly handsome family?

MAUDE

You certainly may; I like to hear it said. I'm sorry our chauffeur couldn't meet you. He was away with Mr. Larrabee.

PAUL
(*With great, happy relief*)
Oh, then that was *not* Fairchild!

MAUDE
(*Puzzled*)
No, it was John, the gardener.

PAUL
Oh, yes, the gardener.

LINUS
(*Examining him carefully*)
How did you know our chauffeur's name was Fairchild?

PAUL
(*Easily*)
I believe your mother said on the telephone that I would
be met by a man named Fairchild. What a lovely place you
have here!
(*He is looking over at the garage.*)

MAUDE
Yes, we're very fond of it. That's Long Island Sound, you
know.

PAUL
Beautiful!
(*But his eyes keep returning to the garage.*)

LINUS
That's the garage.

PAUL

(*Ignoring that one*)

But how lucky you are! It is like having the Riviera an hour from Paris.

MAUDE

Yes, it is. (*And then, in her careful French*) Mais, dites-moi, monsieur, est-ce que vous preferez parler le français?

PAUL

Ah, non, madame, vous êtes très aimable, but I prefer to speak English while I am here. If you can put up with my English.

MAUDE

But it's very good! Did you go to school in England?

PAUL

No, I had an English nanny.

LARRABEE

(*Abruptly*)

Can I get you a drink?

PAUL

Thank you, but I'm afraid it's a bit early in the day for me for spirits.

LARRABEE

Not for me. You'll excuse me.

(*He starts for the bar.*)

MAUDE

(*Gaily*)

Oh, but we'll have an apéritif before lunch! I think some champagne, Linus! (*To* PAUL) There's really no apéritif like champagne, is there? So much nicer than cocktails.

PAUL

I agree, oh yes!

MAUDE

(*Calling*)

Will you see to it, Linus? And to the wine for lunch? (LAR-
RABEE *grunts and goes into the bar*) Now, I know you'll want
to get rid of some of the soot you acquired on the ride out.
Don't you just love our railroad? David, will you take Monsieur d'Argenson up to your room?

> (MARGARET *comes from the house to get the coffee*
> *tray.*)

PAUL

Thank you; you are very kind.

> (*The three men start for the house.*)

DAVID

Did you fly over?

PAUL

Yes. I would have preferred the boat, but there is never
enough time these days, is there?

MAUDE

Margaret, would you tell Fairchild I would like to see him?

> (PAUL's *head almost snaps around, but he holds it as*
> *he sees* LINUS *watching him.* MARGARET *goes off.*)

PAUL

What a magnificent view! And all those boats, they are
yours?

LINUS

Yes, they are.

PAUL

Ah, yes, I have heard you are a great family of sailors.
(*They continue on to the house,* LINUS *a step to the rear.*)

DAVID

Do you sail?

PAUL

No, skiing and shooting are my sports.

LINUS

Tell me: have you ever shot wild boar in Belgium?

PAUL

Oh, yes! Wonderful sport!
(LINUS *nods with satisfaction, and they go into the house.* MAUDE *stands and watches them go, then droops a little and stares out into space, and allows herself, finally, the small, pleasant ache of feeling sorry for herself.* FAIRCHILD *and* MARGARET *appear from the right and approach her, and it is* MARGARET'S *passage to the house that brings* MAUDE *to with a start.*)

MAUDE

Oh! Fairchild. Yes. I want to speak to you. (MARGARET *goes into the house*) Will you sit down? Please. Bring a chair.

FAIRCHILD

No, thank you, madam.
(*She nods and regards him calmly, with instinctive sureness.*)

MAUDE

I have something to tell you that is quite personal, and for the time being I'd rather it weren't discussed in the household. I know I can depend on you. It concerns Mister David and Sabrina. (*His eyes show a flash of anxiety, but his face remains expressionless*) Sabrina hasn't told you.

FAIRCHILD

No, madam.

MAUDE

David came to me this morning and said he wishes to marry Sabrina.

FAIRCHILD

I beg your pardon?

MAUDE

Mr. David wishes to marry Sabrina.
(FAIRCHILD *considers it quietly.* SABRINA *comes dashing on, bubbling over with high spirits. All the doubt and self-searching of the previous evening are gone.*)

SABRINA

Linus? (*At sight of them she stops short*) Oh, I'm sorry. I was looking for Linus.

MAUDE

Sabrina, I've just told your father. (SABRINA *looks blank*) About you and David.

SABRINA

Oh.

MAUDE

I thought I should consult you, Fairchild, as to how we should proceed.

FAIRCHILD

I'm sorry, madam, I won't have it.

MAUDE
(*Startled*)

What?

FAIRCHILD

Begging your pardon, madam, I'll not hear of it.

MAUDE

Oh! Sabrina, perhaps you'd like to speak to your father alone.

SABRINA
(*Quickly*)

Oh, no!

FAIRCHILD

I mean no offense, madam. I've always liked Mr. David.

MAUDE

Yes, Fairchild, of course. I'm not offended that you oppose the marriage. No. But I'm terribly curious to know *why* you oppose it. And I'm sure Sabrina is, too.

FAIRCHILD
(*Simply*)

I couldn't stand the scandal.

MAUDE

Oh.

FAIRCHILD

Please understand, madam. I've worked hard, these thirty years, at the one job I've wanted and I've gained the respect

of my fellow men. And I'll not see it go. There's no credit
for me, or for her, in such a marriage. It's all very well for
you and Mr. Larrabee: the papers and all would say how fine
and democratic you were to be giving your blessing to the
marriage. But nobody would praise Tom Fairchild and call
him a democratic man. No. They'd laugh behind my back.
And it would be no good trying to tell them that I've got
more money than I know how to use in this life. . . .

MAUDE

Have you, Fairchild?

FAIRCHILD

Yes, madam. But they wouldn't believe it. And they
wouldn't care. Democracy can be a wickedly unfair thing,
madam. Nobody poor was ever called democratic for marrying somebody rich.

(*A pause, as* MAUDE *considers that one. Then she
rouses herself.*)

MAUDE

But Fairchild, if the children defy us . . . surely if you
have that much money . . . after all, you love books so
. . . you could retire, and read.

FAIRCHILD

Read on my own time?

(*He shakes his head, dubiously. The door to the bar
opens, and* LARRABEE *walks onto the terrace carrying
a drink half gone. They turn as they hear the door
slam.*)

MAUDE

Oh. Linus.

LARRABEE

Well?

MAUDE

Fairchild won't hear of it.

LARRABEE

What?

MAUDE

He won't have the marriage. He won't hear of it.
(LARRABEE *lets the news sink in. He hefts the glass, examines it carefully, then addresses it.*)

LARRABEE

(Quietly)

I can remember, back in the twenties, when George Bellamy's daughter eloped with the chauffeur. It was on the front pages of every newspaper in the country, and the news was cabled abroad. It shook our world. Now, my son has decided that he wants to marry our chauffeur's daughter. I am forced to approve. My wife pretends to be delighted. But the chauffeur . . . won't hear of it.
(*He drains the glass, then with his toe, he pushes a potted plant off the edge of the terrace. It crashes on the ground below. He turns calmly and goes back into the bar.* MAUDE *immediately starts after him.*)

MAUDE

Linus!

FAIRCHILD

Madam, will you explain to him . . .

141

MAUDE

(*Hastily, as she goes*)

Yes, Fairchild, of course. It's not democratic.

(*She hurries into the bar.* SABRINA, *who had to clap a hand to her mouth at the conclusion of* LARRABEE'S *speech, has now regained control, and she looks at her father with affection.*)

FAIRCHILD

(*Gruffly*)

I'm sorry. I want you to be happy. But I had to say what was in my mind.

(*He turns and goes. And now, as* SABRINA *lets the laughter bubble to the surface, she is close to tears at the same time; wild with rage and wild with laughter at the entire situation. She doubles over with horror and laughter, then straightens up and holds her head.* DAVID *comes out of the house talking to* LINUS, *who follows a few steps behind.*)

DAVID

You certainly were inquisitive. Why all those questions?

LINUS

I wanted to know something about him.

DAVID

Why did you put in a phone call to Paris?

LINUS

I want to know all about him.

DAVID

Why? (*But then he sees* SABRINA, *and stops short, apprehensive at the way she looks at him*) Sabrina, I have to talk to you.

SABRINA
(*Reproachfully*)

Oh, David! David! David!

DAVID
(*Horrified*)

Don't tell me you know!

SABRINA

Know! David! You decided you want to marry me, so you went and asked your mother!

DAVID

Now, wait a minute . . .
(*He hurries to her.*)

SABRINA

And your mother asked your father, and probably your brother, and then went and asked her chauffeur! Who just happens to be my father! There's still the cook and the maid and the upstairs maid and the gardener to ask. When are you going to get around to asking me?

DAVID

Sabrina . . .

LINUS

David, for God's sake!
(*And he is overcome with laughter.*)

DAVID

Now, wait a minute! I don't know how this happened . . .

SABRINA

But I know. It happened because you took me for granted. Oh, yes. Look deep, David. You took it for granted that I would curtsy and say, "Yes, sir," didn't you?

DAVID

No!

(MAUDE *comes out of the bar.*)

SABRINA

Of course you did. It never crossed your mind that I might curtsy and say, "No, sir." But it did cross your mind that your mother might say no. And so, of course you spoke to your mother instead of to me.

DAVID

That's not how it happened! I tried to ask you last night, but you kept changing the subject. And then, this morning . . .

MAUDE

David, do you mean to say you hadn't asked Sabrina? David, how rude!

DAVID

(*Frantic*)

Nobody gave me a chance to ask her! All I did was speak to you out of sheer politeness, because I felt I owed it to you, and the next thing I knew, it was on the agenda of the United Nations!

LINUS

(*Peremptorily*)

Sabrina, what did you find out last night?

SABRINA

What do you care? You took it for granted, too, didn't you?

LINUS
(*After a moment, bluntly*)
Yes.

SABRINA

And that's what's always been wrong with the story. Everyone takes it for granted that Cinderella will marry Prince Charming when he comes knocking on her door with that diamond-studded slipper. Nobody considers Cinderella. What if she thinks Prince Charming is a great big oaf? Ah, not you, David, you're sweet . . .

DAVID
(*Strongly, directly*)
Sabrina, I apologize. I love you. I want to marry you. I want you to marry me. Will you?

SABRINA
(*Trying to smile, she makes a small curtsy*)
No, sir.

DAVID
(*Grimly*)
I don't blame you after this.

SABRINA
(*Tenderly*)
Ah, no, not after this. It's not out of pique; not because I'm offended. Thank you for wanting to marry me, David. And thank you again for a beautiful night, and for the chance to find out what I needed to know. I wanted you very much

to make love to me last night, did you know that? But you were a gentleman, and by the time you felt you knew me well enough to try, I knew you well enough to know I didn't want you to. Ah, is that cruel?

LINUS
(*Sharply*)
You don't know what you're doing.

SABRINA
What?
(*She whirls to face him.*)

LINUS
You've been in love with him all your life.

SABRINA
And I fell out of love in a night.

LINUS
(*Savagely*)
Get rid of those romantic ideas! It doesn't happen that way!
(*She stares at him.*)

SABRINA
Oh? What's the matter? Aren't we making the right moves? Shall I take him, not loving him? Is that being realistic in one easy lesson; is that how you make the game come out? Do you know what I think? I don't think you know how to make it come out! I don't think you have another move left! And what's wrong with Ralph Waldo Emerson?

LINUS
(*Hard*)
You're running away from everything you wanted!

SABRINA

No!

LINUS

All of the world and love!

SABRINA

No!

LINUS

If you settle for Paris, you're lost!

DAVID

(*Cutting in sharply*)

Look, if I'm going to be turned down, let me do it on my own, will you?

LINUS

David, this is important!

DAVID

Why to you?

(*And that stops* LINUS *dead. Pause.* SABRINA *regards him thoughtfully.*)

SABRINA

Yes. Why to you?

(*Pause. Then* LINUS *looks past* SABRINA *to see* PAUL D'ARGENSON *stroll out onto the terrace.*)

LINUS

Miss Fairchild, have you . . .

(*He gestures toward* PAUL. SABRINA *turns and looks, stares in disbelief, and shakes her head in horror.*)

PAUL

'Allo, Sabrina, *ça va?*

SABRINA

Oh, no. Oh, no, no, no, no, no. (*She advances on Paul murderously*) How dare you come across the ocean looking

for me, and walk in on these people you don't even know?
They're having enough trouble with me as it is! Go away! Go
home! Go back to Paris!

PAUL

Mais, ne te faches pas! I wanted to surprise you!

SABRINA

Well, you did!

MAUDE
(*Quietly*)

Sabrina, I think we may assume from this that you and
Monsieur d'Argenson are acquainted. But I really don't like
having my luncheon guests ordered out of my house.

> (*And* SABRINA, *suffused in mortification, stands there
> looking helplessly for something to hold on to. Then
> suddenly she turns, ducks her head, and dashes off
> toward the garage.*)

LINUS

> (*Seeing her heading for the old wooden trellis*)

Look out!

> (*But it is too late. There is a crash, and we hear
> SABRINA'S voice in a tearful wail.*)

SABRINA
(*Off*)

Oh! . . . Ow! . . . Oh!

> LINUS *dashes off toward her, with* PAUL *and* DAVID *right
> after him.*)

The Curtain Falls

ACT FOUR

ACT FOUR

The same, a few seconds later. As the curtain rises, LINUS
strolls on with SABRINA *in his arms.*

MAUDE

Is she all right?

LINUS

No bones broken. But quite a scratch on one leg. (*He
smiles down at* SABRINA) The same leg, I think.

SABRINA

(*Coldly*)
Will you put me down, please?

LINUS

In the same place? It seems appropriate. (*He sets her on
the wall*) There you are.

SABRINA

I'd like to go home, please.
    (DAVID *hurries on with a pail of water.* PAUL *is right
behind him.* LINUS *gets out a clean handkerchief and
dips it in the water.*)

LINUS

Raise your skirt.
    (*No response.*)

PAUL

Sabrina, raise your skirt.
    (LINUS *waits;* SABRINA *stares at him grimly.*)

LINUS

(Good-humored)

Would you rather have David do it? David . . .
> *(He hands her leg to* DAVID, *then the handkerchief.*
> DAVID *holds her leg, then glances at* PAUL, *and hesitates.)*

DAVID

Maybe you'd like to . . .
> *(He pushes the leg toward* PAUL.*)*

PAUL

Thank you. *(He makes a move to take the leg, then remembers that he is a guest)* Oh, no, no. You go ahead.

DAVID

(Insistent)

Here.

PAUL

No, it's perfectly all right.

SABRINA

Would you gentlemen kindly stop passing my leg about among you?
> *(She pulls her leg away, and takes the handkerchief.)*

MAUDE

David, Linus, I think Sabrina and Monsieur d'Argenson would like to talk alone.
> (MARGARET *has appeared on the terrace.)*

MARGARET

Paris is calling Mr. Linus, madam.

MAUDE

Paris? Linus, there's a long distance call for you from . . .

LINUS

Yes, Mother, I'll take it.
> (*He runs across, and up the steps, and into the house.* MARGARET *follows him in, and* MAUDE *starts to follow.*)

MAUDE

David . . . ?
> (DAVID *stares at* PAUL *and* SABRINA *for a moment, then goes into the garden.*)

PAUL
> (*Apologetically*)

Mrs. Larrabee . . .

MAUDE

No, no.
> (*She goes into the house.* PAUL *turns to* SABRINA. *Pause.*)

SABRINA

Hello . . . (*He studies her for a moment, then strides over to her, pulls a small jeweler's box from his pocket, hands it to her, and walks away*) What is it?

PAUL
> (*Diffidently*)

Nothing. A rabbit.
> (*She opens the box and looks.*)

SABRINA

Ah, Paul! A gold rabbit! For my bracelet!
> (*She comes off the wall and goes to him.*)

PAUL
> (*Still slightly injured*)

I thought it might please you.

SABRINA

It does! I love it! Thank you, Paul!
(*He turns and smiles at her.*)

PAUL

But you do not remember what it is.

SABRINA

Should I? Is it something special?

PAUL

Do you remember your birthday last year? In Dijon. We
took a walk in the woods near the house, and when we came
home the little gardener's daughter brought you a present.
A rabbit.

SABRINA

Oh, yes!

PAUL

And you asked her to take care of it for you, and told her
she must call it Peter, because in America all rabbits are
called Peter.

SABRINA

(*Laughing*)

How sweet of you to remember. I wonder how Peter is,
now.

PAUL

Peter is once again a mother. (*She laughs joyously. He
grins*) Push his tail.

SABRINA

Mmm?

PAUL

Yes! Push his tail!
(*She does.*)

SABRINA
(*With delight*)

He wiggles his ears!

PAUL

But a rabbit must wiggle his ears!

SABRINA

How lovely. (*She touches him gently*) Thank you, Paul.
(*Pause.*)

PAUL
(*A little ruefully*)

That was not the welcome I expected.

SABRINA

Oh.

PAUL

One takes a plane because the boat would seem so long,
and looks forward so to the meeting, and then . . . (*He
shrugs*) Go away. Go home. Go back to Paris.

SABRINA

I'm sorry. I was having trouble with a domestic problem,
and I didn't think I'd have to tackle my foreign policy so
soon.

PAUL

And what is the domestic problem?

SABRINA

David wants to marry me.
(*He stares at her for a moment.*)

155

PAUL

You have been a busy girl these two weeks. (*But then he retracts*) No, I can understand his wanting to marry you. But I would not like it if you wanted to marry him.

SABRINA

I don't.

PAUL

It has not gone well, here.

SABRINA
(*Turning away*)

No.

(*He watches her for a moment, then speaks with gentle warmth and possessiveness.*)

PAUL

Sabrina, when you said you must go back to America, I let you go. I did not want to let you go. But I knew it was something you must do, and I thought: "She will come back soon." But it is already too long. And so I have come across the ocean to tell you that I have missed you.

SABRINA
(*Affected and pleased*)

Did you really come all that distance just to see me?

PAUL
(*Nods*)

Paris has not been the same without you.

SABRINA
(*With deep nostalgia*)

Was it lovely the day you left?

PAUL

Yes.

SABRINA

It didn't rain.

PAUL

A little, in the morning.

SABRINA

(*Far away*)

A gray Paris morning . . . and in back of the Madeleine, the old women selling flowers in the rain . . .

PAUL

Will you come home to Paris, Sabrina?

(LINUS *comes out of the house and lopes over to them cheerfully.*)

LINUS

How are you getting along with the patient?

PAUL

Oh, fine! Very well. But I'm afraid it was wrong of Sabrina to mislead your brother so.

LINUS

We always blame the woman when a man falls in love, as though no man had the courage of his inclinations.

PAUL

I beg your pardon?

(SABRINA's *eyes open wide with surprise.*)

SABRINA

Thank you.

LINUS

You're here on business. I may be able to give you a hand.

PAUL

(*A quick wary glance at* SABRINA, *who is tying the handkerchief around her knee, then he smiles at* LINUS)

Why, ah . . . that is very good of you. I know you, of course. Larrabee Shipping. I wish I had a thousand francs for every bill of lading I have paid to Larrabee Lines.

LINUS

I trust we didn't overcharge you.

PAUL

I am your guest, monsieur.

LINUS

(*With an acknowledging nod*)

You're trying to get hold of that new plastic, aren't you? The new process for producing Polyvinyl Chloride.

PAUL

(*Startled*)

How did you know?

LINUS

It's a great formula: cuts the cost in half.

PAUL

(*Grudgingly*)

Well, I thought while I was here . . .

LINUS

You're smart to try to tie up the European rights. You'll make a killing.

158

PAUL

(*Eagerly*)

That I know! But my problem is . . . (*Then, with a glance at* SABRINA, *who is watching grimly*) Ah, well, such a thing is not of great importance . . .

LINUS

It's too bad you found you couldn't do anything about it from Paris. If you had got in touch with me, I'd have saved you the trip.

PAUL

You know the company? (LINUS *nods*) You are not associated with . . . (LINUS *nods*) You do not own it.

LINUS

I will, on Monday.

PAUL

Oh, *mon Dieu!* And I have been trying for four months! Monsieur Larrabee, I do not expect you to take my word that I am the best man in Europe to handle this. I can give you all the references . . .

LINUS

I don't need them. I know you're the man. I've inquired.

PAUL

D'accord?

LINUS

D'accord.

PAUL

Sabrina, did you hear? You have led me to the one man I came to find. You are my good luck; I have known it always.

SABRINA

(Icily)

I'm awfully glad I brought you two together.

PAUL

(Going to her, smiling)

Ah, no, *je t'en prie*, this is something you do not understand.

LINUS

(Easily)

Perhaps I shouldn't have brought up business at this particular time.

PAUL

No, no! Sabrina was making a joke . . .

LINUS

(Going to him)

I'll tell you: my father is chairman of the board and he would want to be consulted on a deal of this sort. He's very much interested in plastics.

PAUL

Yes, I would like to talk to him. He offered me a drink a while ago . . .

LINUS

You'll find him there in the bar having a scoop for himself.

PAUL

(Happily going toward the bar)

Thank you.

LINUS

And then we'll set up a meeting at my office on Monday.

PAUL

You are very kind. (*He smiles at* SABRINA's *back*) Sabrina, you should have told me about him!

(*He salutes* LINUS *and goes into the bar.* LINUS *salutes back, then turns to* SABRINA.)

SABRINA

(*Coldly*)

Congratulations. You did quite a job.

(*She starts for the garage.*)

LINUS

(*Gently*)

Don't run, Sabrina, you've only got one good leg left.

(*She stops and whirls to face him.*)

SABRINA

Why did you do it?

LINUS

Because you curtsied and said no to David.

SABRINA

And what did that mean to you?

LINUS

That I'd underestimated you. If you wouldn't settle for David, you don't have to settle for him.

SABRINA

I would like to decide for myself!

LINUS

I should hate to see you domesticated, Sabrina. There are so many wonderful things you want to do.

SABRINA

Were you afraid I might be forgetting?

LINUS

Stand still and choose, Sabrina. You're so excited by the things you learned in Paris that you're galloping off in all directions. If you want to see everything and do everything and live an active life in a passive world, you'd better get used to the idea that you have to live it alone.

SABRINA

(Desperately)

Why? Why? Suddenly I find you know me better than anyone else in this world—God knows how—but why this terrible compulsion to make me into your own image? If you are the cat that walks alone, must I walk alone, too?

LINUS

Sooner or later you learn that there's a conspiracy of little people in this world to cut you down to their size. And then you grow up and make your choice: to live on their terms or your own. *(Savagely)* You still can marry your Frenchman. Nothing I've done has changed things. You can still have everything money can buy, and ski all over the map of Europe. If you want to sell out, go sell. Just walk through that door and say yes.

SABRINA

How easy for you to make the challenge. *(Flashing out)* Will you give up everything? And start with nothing?

LINUS

Any day! The only measure of living is how productive you are. Don't get that confused with money.

SABRINA

Do you honestly think I have?

SABRINA FAIR

LINUS

(*Taking her by the arm and holding her hard*)

You've discovered that life is an enormous experience that must be used. Are you going to settle for the very best burgundy?

(*Pause.*)

SABRINA

(*Quietly*)

No. No. Would you let go of me, please? (*He makes no move. She disengages herself and steps back*) If I'm to live on my own terms, that is making a start, isn't it?

LINUS

Yes.

SABRINA

And what is the next step?

LINUS

I think you'll learn on your own. You've already made a good start.

SABRINA

Never to let anyone impose his terms on me? Not even you?

LINUS

That's right.

SABRINA

And how shall I prevent it?

LINUS

By imposing your terms on others.

SABRINA

That takes power. (*Pause*) I see. It is the most exciting game in the world, isn't it? With life-size figures. And the one who loves is captured.

LINUS

The answer is: not to love.

SABRINA

And be without love? (*She moves closer.* JULIA *appears from the house and stands on the terrace, watching*) Have you made your choice, Linus? And is it irrevocable? Power corrupts, you know. And absolute power corrupts absolutely.

LINUS

Where did you get that? Out of a book?

SABRINA

(*Softly*)

I beg you to think that you may be mistaken.

JULIA

Why don't you hit him? It's the only thing he'll understand. (*They turn to her. Her eyes are flashing murderously*) What are you trying to do to this girl?

LINUS

How do you know I'm trying to do anything?

JULIA

I have a room with a view! You're afraid to take her, and afraid to lose her, so you're warning her off the rest of the world. I don't have to tell you what you're passing up; it's pretty damned clear you know. But you want to own her without being owned. You can't unbend, you won't give in.

164

You're a stiff-necked, self-sufficient, autocratic bastard . . .
(*She begins to cry*) . . . and you've been my favorite man since
the day you were born.

LINUS
(*Taking a step to her*)

Aunt Julia . . .

JULIA
(*Tearfully*)

If you come near me, I'll kick you. What do you want to
do? Make her a part of Larrabee Industries? And then fight
off your competitors? Just hang a sign around her neck!
"Please don't handle the merchandise!" (*She turns to* SA-
BRINA) And as for you! You listen to me! If anyone tries to
tell you that she travels the farthest who travels alone, believe me, when you get there you'll find it wasn't worth the
trip! (*She turns on* LINUS) Get into her life or get out of her
life! But dont stand around playing God!

(MAUDE *has appeared from the house.*)

MAUDE
(*Concerned*)

Julia, what's the matter?

JULIA

The whole trouble is, you didn't beat him enough!
(*She ducks her head and runs into the house. Pause.*
MAUDE *stares at* LINUS *coldly.*)

MAUDE

Linus, it is almost time for lunch. Have you been sailing,
or are you going sailing?

LINUS

I've been sailing, Mother.

MAUDE

Then it would please me if you would go and change. I'm quite fond of you in that costume, but I prefer something less rakish for lunch.

LINUS

Yes, Mother.

(*He starts for the house.*)

MAUDE

And please tell Margaret we'll have cocktails inside in ten minutes.

LINUS

Yes, Mother.

MAUDE

Your father ordered up a bottle of champagne. I think we'll need two.

LINUS

Yes, Mother.

MAUDE

Where is Monsieur d'Argenson?

LINUS

In the bar, counting his blessings.

(*He goes in.* MAUDE *looks across at* SABRINA.)

MAUDE

I want to apologize. I'm only beginning to realize what we have done to you here, these past two weeks.

SABRINA

Ah, no, please. It's nobody's fault but my own. (*And then, almost to herself*) How silly to think that since I had changed, the world must have changed along with me.

MAUDE

My world is so rigid, and has such a horror of change. I didn't make the rules I live by. I suppose it's cowardly of me to say that, but it's true. They were made for me before I was born.

SABRINA

(*With a wry smile*)
You forget, I was brought up by those very same rules.

MAUDE

But with none of the fun or advantages. And yet, when you had a chance to move into this world, you said no. (*A moment*) You knew I didn't want you to marry David.

SABRINA

I guessed.

MAUDE

(MAUDE *regards the girl thoughtfully, then decides to say what she must say as lightly as she can*)
You know . . . most people think of Mr. Larrabee as a quite charming but rather stuffy old gentleman; and they think that I am bright, and broad-minded, and . . . "liberal." You think that, don't you? It's not true. He and I are very much alike; it's why we've got along. I believe, as he does, that the world we were brought up in was the way the world was meant to be. That world started to come to an end when we were very young—oh, as early as 1914, I suppose—and it has been struggling for its life ever since. He feels more strongly than I do. He says the death-blow came at the end of the nineteen-twenties, and that we live on in a cemetery, decorating the graves. I don't like to think that; I won't go to the funerals. But I do think that the world has become . . . un-

satisfactory. I trust that the next will have more grace and dignity. (*She tosses her head with a small, charming smile of defiance*) If it doesn't, I shall speak sharply to the proprietor.

SABRINA

(*Genuinely*)

I hope it does, for you.

MAUDE

Let's all hope. And still, there are many pleasant things that remain, and I want to hold on to them; for myself, for as long as I can, and for David.

SABRINA

You adore David.

MAUDE

He's very much like me. And the things I want for him are the things he wants for himself: a calm, orderly world, the pursuit of comfort; the avoidance of pain. Is that what you want? (SABRINA *shakes her head*) I think it's rather bright of me to see that. Well, then, you're free of our world. Just as Linus is. And if money means that little to you, you're safe. (*Pause*) Well? Since you dislike me heartily, now, will you at least say, when you speak of this, that I was honest?

SABRINA

I like you very much.

> (*They smile at each other fondly, and then the woman takes the girl in her arms and holds her in a long embrace.*)

MAUDE

I wish you had been my daughter.

> (SABRINA, *moved, crinkles up her eyes with pleasure.* LARRABEE *comes striding out of the bar.*)

LARRABEE

Maude! Maude!

MAUDE

(Exasperated)

Oh, Linus, I do wish you'd give up calling me from long distances!

(LINUS strolls out of the house.)

LARRABEE

Maude, we've got a very strange Frenchman on our hands. He's fallen madly in love with Linus. *(To LINUS)* What did you do to him?

LINUS

Gave him some money.

LARRABEE

(That's understandable)

Oh. Well. But he's quite an interesting chap. Did you know that they still use horses in France for funerals? In the small towns, that is.

(During the discourse on horses in France, DAVID appears from the garden, holding FAIRCHILD firmly by the elbow, hustling him along. He is alive with delight and excitement. FAIRCHILD is definitely reluctant.)

FAIRCHILD

Please, Mr. David, if you don't mind . . .

DAVID

You can't keep a thing like that secret! Now don't move. *(He plants FAIRCHILD, and turns on SABRINA with a wide grin)* Sabrina, your father just came to tell me that he's sorry he turned me down. He's decided he mustn't stand in the way of our happiness.

SABRINA

Oh!

DAVID

But then I told him that you had turned me down, and he thinks it may be because of money. He thinks you might change your mind if you had some money of your own. Is that true?

SABRINA

No.

DAVID

I didn't think so. (*He turns on Fairchild*) But it still holds. You're not going to back down.

FAIRCHILD

(*Worried*)

No, sir, but . . .

LARRABEE

(*To* MAUDE)

Did she turn him down, too? What's wrong with the boy?

DAVID

(*Grinning*)

I'm just not the guy, Father. That sort of thing does happen. Even to us. All right, Fairchild.

FAIRCHILD

I'd rather not speak of it now, sir . . .

DAVID

Don't be so modest! (*He races to* SABRINA, *takes her by the shoulders, and sits her down*) Sabrina, you're going to learn something about yourself, and it may come as a shock. But no matter what, remember, I liked you for yourself.

(*He runs into the garden.* FAIRCHILD *turns to him as he goes.*)

FAIRCHILD

Mr. David . . .

DAVID

You're on your own, Fairchild!
(*He runs off. Pause.*)

LARRABEE

Well, what is it?
(*And* FAIRCHILD, *trapped, faces the situation, composes himself as best he can, and addresses the family with simple dignity.*)

FAIRCHILD

I have told Mr. David that I would like to settle some money on Sabrina.

MAUDE

Ah, that's very sweet, Fairchild, but I'm sure Sabrina wouldn't dream of taking your life's savings.

FAIRCHILD
(*Quietly*)

I would like her to have something of her own, now.

LARRABEE

That's damned decent, Fairchild. What kind of sum did you have in mind?

FAIRCHILD
(*Simply*)

Five hundred thousand dollars.

LARRABEE
(*Impassively*)

Five hundred thousand dollars.

FAIRCHILD

Yes, sir.

LARRABEE

You saved that out of your salary?

FAIRCHILD

Oh, no, sir, I made investments. I'd rather not talk about it . . .

LARRABEE
(*Suddenly enraged*)

You've run up investments of half a million dollars, and you'd rather not talk about it?
(*He starts across to* FAIRCHILD.)

MAUDE

Now, Linus, be calm!

LARRABEE

How the hell could a man in your position . . .
(LINUS *cuts across swiftly, blocks off his father, and regards him calmly.*)

LINUS
(*Quietly*)

Do you mind? (*He turns to* FAIRCHILD) Fairchild, this is all in the family. I'd like to know how you did it.

FAIRCHILD

It wasn't difficult, sir. I came here to drive for your father shortly after I came out of the army, in 1919. And by 1926, Della and I had saved six thousand dollars. And it occurred to me to buy some stocks. At first I bought them outright, but then one day I overheard Mr. Larrabee explain to Mrs. Larrabee why it showed confidence in our country to buy

172

on margin. So, from then on, I did. I was driving you to New-
port at the time, I believe, sir.

LINUS

And things went along well.

FAIRCHILD

Yes, sir. Since I invested only in companies I had personal
confidence in. Like General Motors. But finally, I began to
worry. It didn't seem right to be getting all that money for
doing something that any fool could do. And it seemed rather
a revolting spectacle to see money making money, like small
animals breeding in dark corners. I beg your pardon, madam.
(*To* LINUS) And so I sold out.

LINUS

When did you sell out?

FAIRCHILD

Early in October, 1929.
(LINUS *has to work hard to keep from laughing.* LAR-
RABEE *looks murderous.*)

MAUDE

But Fairchild! You could have retired! You didn't have to
work here!

FAIRCHILD
(*Mopping his brow*)
But I *wanted* to work here!

LINUS
(*Back to him*)
And so you sold out, put your money in the bank, and
never went near the market again.

173

FAIRCHILD

No, sir, I went back in. This is very difficult, Mr. Linus.

LINUS

Well, here, sit down.
> (*He moves in a chair.*)

FAIRCHILD

Thank you, sir.
> (*He sits.*)

LINUS

So you went back into the market.

FAIRCHILD

Yes, sir. In 1932. I was sorry to see the stocks of such fine companies fallen so low. I felt I should help by buying as much as I could.

LARRABEE

> (*Howling*)

Oh, that was good of you!

FAIRCHILD

But this time, I didn't buy on margin. I bought the stocks and put them away.

LINUS

What about the revolting spectacle of money making money, like small animals breeding in dark corners?

FAIRCHILD

I overcame my revulsion, sir. Then, too, I wanted to show my loyalty to the family in its time of trouble.

LARRABEE
(*Alert*)

What do you mean?

FAIRCHILD

The family firm was in quite some difficulties at the time, sir. As you may remember. Mr. Linus was still in college, and had not yet come into the firm.

LARRABEE

Don't rub it in.

LINUS
(*Cutting in*)
And so to show your loyalty to the family, you . . .

FAIRCHILD

Yes, sir. I bought some Larrabee Shipping.

LINUS

How much?

FAIRCHILD

Seven thousand shares.

LINUS

Seven thou . . . ! (*And now he drives on with intensity*) Fairchild. Those seven thousand shares. You kept them. You put them away.

FAIRCHILD

Yes, sir.

LINUS

And after I came into the company, and we began to expand into other things: every time I split that stock, every time I recapitalized, you went along.

FAIRCHILD

I had great confidence in you, Mr. Linus.

LINUS

And you still own it all.

FAIRCHILD

Yes, sir.

LINUS

(*Driving on*)

Fairchild, you don't have to answer this. Would it be presumptuous of me to suggest that you are worth around a million dollars?

FAIRCHILD

That is true, sir.

LINUS

Am I pushing you too hard if I suggest that it is over a million?

FAIRCHILD

When I last looked, it was *just* over a million, sir.

LARRABEE

Fairchild, you're fired!

FAIRCHILD

(*Injured*)

I hope you don't mean that sir. *I* didn't want to speak of it.

MAUDE

Oh, no, Fairchild, I'm really provoked at you! Think of your family! Think of what you could have done for Della and Sabrina!

176

FAIRCHILD

If Della had lived, madam, I know I'd have done something about it. But most of this happened after she died. And I was happy here. But you may be right about Sabrina.
(*He looks at his daughter.*)

SABRINA

(*Happily, quite overcome with love and laughter*)
I wouldn't have wanted it any other way. (*And then she can't help it: she runs to him and holds him tight*) Bless you.
(FAIRCHILD *disengages, rather embarrassed.*)

FAIRCHILD

(*To* MAUDE)
You'll excuse me, madam. (*To* SABRINA) Whatever you chose to do, the money's yours.

SABRINA

Thank you, Father. It'll come in handy.
(FAIRCHILD *goes. Dead silence. Then* LARRABEE *turns, suddenly, and crosses swiftly to the bar.*)

MAUDE

Linus!

LARRABEE

For thirty years he sat in the front seat, and never gave me a tip.
(*He goes into the bar.*)

SABRINA

(*With a wide, rueful, despairing smile*)
What do you know! I'm an heiress!

MAUDE

How wonderful for you, Sabrina! But you must be careful, now, not to let anyone marry you for your money.

177

SABRINA

(*Laughing*)

I won't. Besides, I'm beginning to think the world is divided into two kinds of men: those you can marry and don't want to; those you want to marry and can't.

MAUDE

(*Suspecting*)

Is there someone you want to marry?

SABRINA

Yes.

MAUDE

Who is it?

SABRINA

(*Turning to* LINUS)

Him.

LINUS

For God's sake, Sabrina, watch your grammar.

SABRINA

It is he.

MAUDE

(MARGARET *appears on the terrace*)

Yes, Margaret, thank you. (MARGARET *goes*) Sabrina, if I were your mother I would oppose this vigorously. But since I am Linus' mother, I'm going in to drink a glass of champagne. (*Before she enters the house, she pauses to look back at them*) It should be interesting, Linus. You want to conquer the world; she wants to love it to death. (*She considers for a moment*) Either way, it'll be an improvement.

    (*She goes in. Pause.* SABRINA *moves down to the hassock, and sits.*)

LINUS
    (*After a long moment, softly*)
How's your knee?

    (*No answer. He crosses to her, takes the bloodstained handkerchief from her, puts it in his pocket, takes out a clean handkerchief, and kneels before her. He waits; she raises her skirt. He swabs the wound, then forms the handkerchief into a bandage, and ties it about her knee, and his hands rest there for a long moment. He looks up. Somehow, although it does not seem as though she has moved, their heads are closer together than before, and it seems impossible not to kiss. They do, gently and briefly, then part. He doesn't move a muscle, but one senses that if he were to let go, he would quiver like a stuck pig. A moment, then he lowers the skirt over her knee, rises and moves away.*)

SABRINA
Haven't you the courage of your inclinations, Linus? (*No answer*) Won't you incline my way?

LINUS
    (*With a glint of a smile*)
Sabrina, you keep forgetting one thing: you don't have to marry anyone.

SABRINA
Oh, yes! I'm not the kind to be alone. I should always have a husband or a small animal about.

LINUS

I'm sure mother would give you back your singing cocka-too.

SABRINA

But his talents are so limited! Will you marry me, Linus? No! Wait! Don't answer that! I'm ahead of myself!

LINUS
(*Grinning*)

I think so, too.

SABRINA
(*Taking a deep breath*)

Linus. Do you love me?

LINUS

You're so peremptory, Sabrina!

SABRINA

Do you?

LINUS
(*Peremptorily*)

Yes!
(*She sighs with relief.*)

SABRINA

Ah, that's good! (*But then she looks anxious*) But you don't believe in marriage.

LINUS

Yes, I do. It's why I've never married.
(*She looks over at him with deep, happy love.*)

SABRINA

That's terribly romantic!

LINUS

Is it? (*He's rather startled*) Yes, it is. But Sabrina, I was never so romantic, or so ambitious, as to aspire to the richest chauffeur's daughter in the world.

SABRINA

You mustn't make fun of my new position in life. It would be the climax to your career. Linus, will you marry me?

LINUS

If mother is right: if I want to take the world with power, and you want to take it with love, which of us will conquer the world, you or I?

SABRINA

(*Moving to him*)

Neither of us . . . alone.

LINUS

And that's why I should marry you.

SABRINA

That . . . and because when you put your hand on my knee, you shook . . . a little. Because power needs the leavening of love, and I love you. (*She looks up at him worshipfully*) Ah, Linus, we couldn't go wrong together. I know. I know that there's nothing, really, in this world we couldn't do together.

LINUS

Even to putting a bottle of the best burgundy on every table, and a tin of pâté de foie gras on every shelf?

SABRINA

Maybe even that.

(A moment and then he takes her and lifts her and sets her on the wall and looks at her with a small, enveloping smile.)

LINUS

"Sabrina Fair, listen where thou are sitting, Under the glassy, cool, translucent wave" . . . do I have it right?

SABRINA

Yes.

LINUS

Sabrina, will you save me from a fate worse than death?

SABRINA

(Softly)

What?

LINUS

(With a trace of a grin)

To be domesticated?

SABRINA

Ah, I thought you might say: to be without love.

LINUS

And that, too. Will you save me, Sabrina? You are the only one who can.

SABRINA

(With a loving smile)

"Gentle swain . . . at thy request . . . I am here."

(He leans forward and takes her in his arms.)

The Curtain Falls